D1418409

EXPLORING

SCIENCE AND MEDICAL DISCOVERIES

Evolution

·EXPLORING·

SCIENCE AND MEDICAL DISCOVERIES

Evolution

**Other books in the
Exploring Science and Medical Discoveries series:**

·EXPLORING·

SCIENCE AND MEDICAL DISCOVERIES

Evolution

Clay Farris Naff, *Book Editor*

Bruce Glassman, *Vice President*
Bonnie Szumski, *Publisher*
Helen Cothran, *Managing Editor*
David M. Haugen, *Series Editor*

GREENHAVEN PRESS
An imprint of Thomson Gale, a part of The Thomson Corporation

THOMSON
™
GALE

Detroit • New York • San Francisco • San Diego • New Haven, Conn.
Waterville, Maine • London • Munich

THOMSON

—————✦—————™

GALE

© 2005 Thomson Gale, a part of The Thomson Corporation.

Thomson and Star Logo are trademarks and Gale and Greenhaven Press are registered trademarks used herein under license.

For more information, contact
Greenhaven Press
27500 Drake Rd.
Farmington Hills, MI 48331-3535
Or you can visit our Internet site at http://www.gale.com

LIBRARY OF CONGRESS CATALOGING-IN-PUBLICATION DATA

Evolution / Clay Farris Naff, book editor.
   p. cm. — (Exploring science and medical discoveries)
  Includes bibliographical references and index.
  ISBN 0-7377-2823-X (lib. : alk. paper)
    1. Evolution (Biology) 2. Evolution (Biology)—History. I. Naff, Clay Farris.
  II. Series.
  QH366.2.E8458   2005
  576.8—dc22
                                          2004060590

Printed in the United States of America

CONTENTS

theory explains how complex organs such as the eye can develop through variation and natural selection. Small, beneficial mutations passed down to future generations can, he says, eventually produce such amazing structures.

4. How Early Bacteria Jump-Started Evolution

A renowned biologist and her son describe the profound influence bacteria have had on the course of evolution. Starting about 2 billion years ago, certain microbes began to use water for fuel, and in the process, they transformed the earth's atmosphere and gave evolution a boost.

5. Tracing Humanity's Origins

A famed fossil hunter and his coauthor describe the search for humanity's origins among hominid fossils. They conclude that humans are members of the ape family.

Chapter 3: Contemporary Controversies

1. Evolution Is Unscientific

A leading advocate of biblical creationism explains why in his view the theory of evolution is unscientific. No one has observed evolutionary processes at work, he contends, and the fossil record fails to support the theory.

2. Evolution Is a Creation Myth

Scientists who buy into evolution's basic assumptions are swallowing a creation myth, argues a law professor who is a leader of the intelligent design movement.

ost great science and medical discoveries emerge slowly from the work of generations of scientists. In their laboratories, far removed from the public eye, scientists seek cures for human diseases, explore more efficient methods to feed the world's hungry, and develop technologies to improve quality of life. A scientist, trained in the scientific method, may spend his or her entire career doggedly pursuing a goal such as a cure for cancer or the invention of a new drug. In the pursuit of these goals, most scientists are single-minded, rarely thinking about the moral and ethical issues that might arise once their new ideas come into the public view. Indeed, it could be argued that scientific inquiry requires just that type of objectivity.

Moral and ethical assessments of scientific discoveries are quite often made by the unscientific—the public—sometimes for good, sometimes for ill. When a discovery is unveiled to society, intense scrutiny often ensues. The media report on it, politicians debate how it should be regulated, ethicists analyze its impact on society, authors vilify or glorify it, and the public struggles to determine whether the new development is friend or foe. Even without fully understanding the discovery or its potential impact, the public will often demand that further inquiry be stopped. Despite such negative reactions, however, scientists rarely quit their pursuits; they merely find ways around the roadblocks.

Embryonic stem cell research, for example, illustrates this tension between science and public response. Scientists engage in embryonic stem cell research in an effort to treat diseases such as Parkinson's and diabetes that are the result of cellular dysfunction. Embryonic stem cells can be derived from early-stage embryos, or blastocysts, and coaxed to form any kind of human cell or tissue. These can then be used to replace damaged or diseased tissues in those suffering from intractable diseases. Many researchers believe that the use of embryonic stem cells to treat human diseases promises to be one of the most important advancements in medicine.

However, embryonic stem cell experiments are highly controversial in the public sphere. At the center of the tumult is the fact that in order to create embryonic stem cell lines, human embryos must be destroyed. Blastocysts often come from fertilized eggs that are left over from fertility treatments. Critics argue that since blastocysts have the capacity to grow into human beings, they should be granted the full range of rights given to all humans, including the right not to be experimented on. These analysts contend, therefore, that destroying embryos is unethical. This argument received attention in the highest office of the United States. President George W. Bush agreed with the critics, and in August 2001 he announced that scientists using federal funds to conduct embryonic stem cell research would be restricted to using existing cell lines. He argued that limiting research to existing lines would prevent any new blastocysts from being destroyed for research.

Scientists have criticized Bush's decision, saying that restricting research to existing cell lines severely limits the number and types of experiments that can be conducted. Despite this considerable roadblock, however, scientists quickly set to work trying to figure out a way to continue their valuable research. Unsurprisingly, as the regulatory environment in the United States becomes restrictive, advancements occur elsewhere. A good example concerns the latest development in the field. On February 12, 2004, professor Hwang Yoon-Young of Hanyang University in Seoul, South Korea, announced that he was the first to clone a human embryo and then extract embryonic stem cells from it. Hwang's research means that scientists may no longer need to use blastocysts to perform stem cell research. Scientists around the world extol the achievement as a major step in treating human diseases.

The debate surrounding embryonic stem cell research illustrates the moral and ethical pressure that the public brings to bear on the scientific community. However, while nonexperts often criticize scientists for not considering the potential negative impact of their work, ironically the public's reaction against such discoveries can produce harmful results as well. For example, although the outcry against embryonic stem cell research in the United States has resulted in fewer embryos being destroyed, those with Parkinson's, such as actor Michael J. Fox, have argued that prohibiting the development of new stem cell lines ultimately will prevent a timely cure for the disease that is killing Fox and thousands of others.

Greenhaven Press's Exploring Science and Medical Discoveries series explores the public uproar that often follows the disclosure of scientific advances in fields such as stem cell research. Each anthology traces the history of one major scientific or medical discovery, investigates society's reaction to the breakthrough, and explores potential new applications and avenues of research. Primary sources provide readers with eyewitness accounts of crucial moments in the discovery process, and secondary sources offer historical perspectives on the scientific achievement and society's reaction to it. Volumes also contain useful research tools, including an introductory essay providing important context, and an annotated table of contents enabling students to quickly locate selections of interest. A thorough index helps readers locate content easily, a detailed chronology helps students trace the history of the discovery, and an extensive bibliography guides readers interested in pursuing further research.

Greenhaven Press's Exploring Science and Medical Discoveries series provides readers with inspiring accounts of how generations of scientists made the world's great discoveries possible and investigates the tremendous impact those innovations have had on the world.

INTRODUCTION

I n the history of controversial scientific theories, evolution drew neither the first nor the fiercest criticism. In 1633, for example, the great Italian scientist Galileo Galilei was hauled before the Inquisition for supporting the Copernican theory that the earth revolves around the sun. Catholic doctrine then held that the sun and all the stars and planets circled the earth daily. Under threat of execution, Galileo renounced his belief in heliocentric theory and meekly accepted house arrest for the remainder of his life.

Charles Darwin never suffered persecution such as Galileo experienced. Yet no concept in science has encountered broader or more prolonged resistance than his theory of evolution. Likewise, none has been more vigorously and steadfastly defended by the global scientific community. An exploration of the history and reasons for this enduring conflict may offer a better understanding of evolution itself.

Darwin's Book Sparks Debate

The battle over evolution began almost immediately following the November 1859 publication of Darwin's landmark book *On the Origin of Species by Means of Natural Selection.* In it he laid out a simple argument derived from these observations: First, offspring are like but not identical to their parents; second, in each generation, far more offspring are born than will survive to reproduce; and third, those individuals whose particular traits help them to leave descendants will tend to pass on those traits to their offspring. Summarizing his argument, Darwin wrote:

> If during the long course of ages and under varying conditions of life, organic beings vary at all in the several parts of their organisation . . . [and] if there be, owing to the high geometrical powers of increase of each species, at some age, season, or year, a severe struggle for life . . . then . . . I think it would be a most extraordinary fact if no variation ever had occurred useful to each being's own welfare, in the same way as so many variations [in domesti-

cated plants or animals] have occurred useful to man. But if variations useful to any organic being do occur, assuredly individuals thus characterised will have the best chance of being preserved in the struggle for life; and from the strong principle of inheritance they will tend to produce offspring similarly characterised. This principle of preservation, I have called, for the sake of brevity, Natural Selection.[1]

Over long periods of time, Darwin claimed, natural selection would create whole new species, each adapted to its particular environment.

The book sold out its first edition within weeks and continued to sell well with every reprinting. This did not, however, signal universal acceptance. On the contrary, many were offended by its implication of an *undirected* process in nature. According to one of Darwin's defenders, critics subjected Darwin to "misrepresentation, ridicule, and denunciation."[2]

Creationists React

Creationism was the dominant view of the time both in scientific and religious circles, and it had many defenders. Samuel Wilberforce, bishop of Oxford, England, was among the most influential and vociferous denouncers of Darwin's theory. He made no secret of the grounds of his objection. Evolution, as Wilberforce saw it, was an affront to human dignity and religious faith:

> Man's derived supremacy over the earth; man's power of articulate speech; man's gift of reason; man's free will and responsibility; man's fall and man's redemption; the incarnation of the Eternal Son; the indwelling of the Eternal Spirit—all are equally and utterly irreconcilable with the degrading notion of the brute origin of him who was created in the image of God, and redeemed by the Eternal Son assuming to himself His nature. Equally inconsistent . . . with the whole scheme of God's dealings with man as recorded in His word, is Mr. Darwin's daring notion of man's further development . . . through natural selection.[3]

Creation-minded scientists, too, were reluctant to embrace evolution. In America, Louis Agassiz, a Swiss-born professor of natural history at Harvard University, led the resistance to Darwin's theory. Speaking before the Boston Society of Natural History in 1860, Agassiz dismissed evolution as a fad that he hoped to outlive. This was not to be. Years later, near the end of his life, as evolution continued to gain acceptance among scientists, Agassiz again tried to discredit it. In an 1874 *Atlantic Monthly* article, he wrote, "Darwin's works and those of his followers have added nothing new to our previous knowledge concerning the origin of man and his associates in domestic life, the horse, the cow, the sheep, the dog, or indeed, of any animal."[4] Agassiz was not merely interested in critiquing the shortcomings of Darwin's theory. He sought to uphold creationism:

> Have those who object to repeated acts of creation ever considered that no progress can be made in knowledge without repeated acts of thinking? And what are thoughts but specific acts of the mind? Why should it then be unscientific to infer that the facts of nature are the result of a similar process, since there is no evidence of any other cause?[5]

Evolution Gains Adherents

If some religious and scientific leaders found evolution impossible to accept, many others embraced it. According to historian Ronald L. Numbers, before Darwin's death in 1882 evolution "had captivated most British and American scientists, and was beginning to draw favorable comment from religious leaders on both sides of the Atlantic."[6] A prominent colleague of Agassiz at Harvard, botanist Asa Gray, was among the first to accept Darwin's theory. In an 1860 review, Gray endorsed Darwin's views: "Is there anything in Nature which in the long-run may answer to artificial selection? Mr. Darwin thinks that there is; and Natural Selection is the keynote of his discourse. . . . [W]e are ready to adopt the probable conclusion."[7]

No one was more enthusiastic for Darwin's theory than Thomas Huxley, a British professor of natural history. In an 1859 letter to Darwin, Huxley declared himself ready to "go to the stake"[8] if necessary in defense of the new theory. So vigorous and effective was Huxley's advocacy for evolution that he came to be known as Darwin's Bulldog.

That reputation was sealed on June 30, 1860, when Huxley engaged in an impromptu debate with Wilberforce. The exchange took place at the Oxford University Museum. No transcript exists, but by all accounts it was a heated affair. Legend has it that the bishop asked Huxley whether he claimed descent from an ape on his grandfather's or his grandmother's side. To which Huxley is said to have retorted that he would rather have "a miserable ape for a grandfather"[9] than a man who merely ridiculed new ideas.

Evolution continued to rouse strong emotions, spurred on by Darwin's later book, *The Descent of Man*, published in 1871. Within the scientific community Darwin's arguments attracted considerable support, yet his theory remained incomplete. Darwin admitted that he lacked an explanation for how variations and inheritance worked. In a letter to Huxley, he wrote, "what the devil determines each particular variation?"[10]

Darwin died not knowing that the beginnings of an answer had been published by Gregor Mendel, an obscure monk, just a few years after *On the Origin of Species*. Mendel formulated ideas about inheritance from his efforts propagating peas. In 1900 three scientists, having rediscovered Mendel's work, launched the new science of genetics. At last the laws, if not the precise mechanisms, of inheritance became clear. That development, along with rapidly expanding evidence of the immense age of the earth and diversity of its life, spurred evolution into college and high school science curricula.

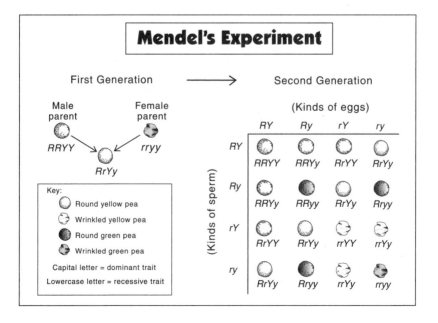

The Rise of Creationist Influence

In the United States opposition grew. A spate of books and pamphlets asserted that the earth's natural history could be interpreted to support the Bible's version of events. The leading actors of this emerging fundamentalist movement were people whose scientific training was trumped by their theological commitments. George Frederick Wright, a geologist who had long accepted evolution, turned his back on Darwinism in the 1890s and went on to become a popular antievolutionist author and editor of a fundamentalist magazine called the *Bible Student and Teacher.*

He was followed by geologist George McCready Price, a Seventh Day Adventist who became known in the 1920s as "the most innovative and influential defender of special creation."[11] Price was a leading proponent of "catastrophism," an interpretation of the geological record as reflecting great biblical events such as Noah's Flood. Rejected by the scientific mainstream, these views nevertheless had enormous influence in American culture. They set the stage for a memorable clash in the courts.

In 1925 the Tennessee legislature passed a law prohibiting the teaching of evolution in public colleges and universities. Later that year a schoolteacher named John T. Scopes stood trial in Dayton, Tennessee, on a charge of teaching evolution. On the prosecution team was three-time presidential candidate and fundamentalist crusader William Jennings Bryan. His 1921 tract *The Menace of Darwinism* had made him a star of the creationist movement.

The defense was led by Clarence Darrow, a brilliant, agnostic lawyer who used the extraordinary tactic of putting Bryan on the witness stand. The trial attracted international attention, and the conviction of Scopes (though later overturned on a technicality) led to a muffling of evolution in the public schools for more than fifty years.

The Sputnik Scare

Public attitudes began to change in 1957, when the Soviet Union launched *Sputnik*, the first earth-orbiting satellite. Many Americans viewed the Soviet accomplishment as evidence of their superior scientific and technological know-how, capabilities that many feared could be used to create weapons to be used against the United States. Suddenly, science education appeared to many

Americans to be a vital part of national defense. The teaching of evolution revived. So, too, did opposition to it. In 1961 evangelist John C. Whitcomb Jr. and civil engineer Henry M. Morris, both well-educated men with a passion for Bible studies, published *The Genesis Flood*, a book that urged fidelity to the biblical narrative no matter what contrary evidence scientists discovered. An instant hit in conservative religious circles, it became the basis for modern "creation science."[12]

Meanwhile, among scientists evolutionary studies were flourishing in the wake of the 1953 discovery of DNA's structure. With a growing understanding of genetics, confidence in evolution's validity soared, and the push to teach the theory grew.

Things came to a head in 1968, when the U.S. Supreme Court struck down state laws banning the teaching of evolution. In a case originating in Arkansas, the Court found that the ban violated the First Amendment's requirement that government remain neutral in religious matters. The Court noted, "The overriding fact is that Arkansas' law . . . proscribes [evolution] for the sole reason that it is deemed to conflict with a particular religious doctrine; that is, with a particular interpretation of the Book of Genesis by a particular religious group."[13]

Thwarted in their efforts to ban the teaching of evolution, creationists founded research institutes, published books claiming the demise of Darwinism, and sought "equal time" laws in state legislatures. Such laws held that educators had to devote equal time to the teaching of creationism and evolution.

Scientists banded together in defense of evolution. In 1981 they formed the National Center for Science Education (NCSE) to preserve, as they put it, the integrity of science education. Those with literary gifts, like paleontologist Stephen Jay Gould and zoologist Richard Dawkins, began to pen books explaining evolution to the general public.

In an extraordinary gesture of scientific solidarity, seventy-two Nobel laureate scientists joined a lawsuit challenging Louisiana's equal time law. In 1987 the Supreme Court ruled that as creation science was not science at all, the equal time approach "impermissibly endorses religion by advancing the religious belief that a supernatural being created humankind."[14]

Denied but not disheartened, creationists soon undertook a new campaign against evolution under the rubric of "intelligent design" or "ID" for short. According to the Center for Science and Culture

(CSC), widely acknowledged as the ID movement's headquarters, "The theory of intelligent design holds that certain features of the universe and of living things are best explained by an intelligent cause, not an undirected process such as natural selection."[15] Intelligent design advocates, perhaps in deference to the Supreme Court, do not generally name the "intelligent cause."

In contrast to biblical literalists, such as those based at the Institute for Creation Research, most ID proponents grant that the earth is more than 4 billion years old and that natural geologic forces, not a great flood, account for its topography. However, they staunchly oppose evolution.

Few scientists have been persuaded to this position. According to the pro-evolution Web site Talkdesign.org, the ratio of evolutionists to ID adherents is more than a hundred to one.[16] According to science journalist Richard Monastersky, to date only one intelligent design paper has been published in a peer-reviewed scientific journal, and that paper, by a philosopher on the Center for Science and Culture staff, was immediately repudiated as an error by the journal's oversight board.[17]

Kenneth R. Miller, a biologist and theist, has summed up the view of the majority of scientists in his field: "In the final analysis, the biochemical hypothesis of intelligent design fails not because the scientific community is closed to it but rather for the most basic of reasons—because it is overwhelmingly contradicted by the scientific evidence."[18]

Grounds for Conflict

The question remains why the theory of evolution continues to generate heated debate while other scientific theories with theological implications, such as heliocentricity, stir little public attention. One reason is that, like Bishop Wilberforce, many opponents see acceptance of evolution as fatal to belief in the Bible's account of human origins. Law professor Philip E. Johnson, whose 1991 book *Darwin on Trial* launched the ID movement, puts it this way: "Darwinistic evolution would be a most peculiar creative method for God to choose given the Darwinistic insistence that biological evolution was *undirected*. . . . How then did God ensure that humans would come into existence so that salvation history would have a chance to occur?"[19]

It must be noted that not all religious people find such questions problematic. Indeed, most evolutionists are also theists. A 2001 Gallup poll of Americans found that 49 percent agreed that humans developed over millions of years (compared with 45 percent who said God created humans in their present form some ten thousand years ago). However, of that 49 percent, three-quarters chose the view that God guided the evolution of humans.[20] Clearly, then, belief in God alone does not entail a rejection of evolution. Although religion nearly always underlies the opposition at some level, other factors must be considered.

First, there is human dignity. Many people find the idea that humans are merely another species of animal, sharing common ancestors with chimpanzees, gorillas, and other great apes, deeply troubling.

Morality comes into play as well. Some critics feel that evolution opens the way to terrible injustices. Don Boys, a fundamentalist preacher and former *USA Today* columnist, sums up this view: "Evolutionary teachings have resulted in soaking the soil of Europe in innocent blood. After all, evolutionists tell us that man is only a little higher than the animals rather than a little lower than the angels as the Bible teaches, so what's a few million lives to be concerned about?"[21] There is some historical basis for this fear. In the late nineteenth century philosophers such as Herbert Spencer and Friedrich Nietzsche transformed Darwin's ideas about "survival of the fittest" to suggest that the rule of strong people over weak people was simply nature's way.

Biologists have long sought to correct the erroneous understanding of that unfortunate phrase. In evolution, fitness refers only to the question of what traits will best serve to pass genes along to future generations. Napoléon Bonaparte (1769–1821) provides an apt example of how Darwin's interpretation of "survival of the fittest" cannot be made to square with Spencer's or Nietzsche's views. Napoléon was the most powerful man in Europe, yet, so far as is known, he fathered just one child, making him evolutionarily less fit than most of the soldiers in the armies he commanded.

Nevertheless, "social Darwinism" and its offshoots were used to justify terrible acts of cruelty and neglect. With the advent of genetics, social Darwinism evolved into the eugenics movement, in which people deemed "unfit" were involuntarily sterilized and eventually, during the Nazi regime in Germany, murdered. Darwin's theory continues to be blamed for such abuses.

Yet history shows that evolution has no special ability to promote evil, the theory's proponents point out. Genocidal wars long predate Darwin. Moreover, the Christian Crusades and Muslim conquests indicate that religion can inspire as well as restrain war. The Soviet rejection of Darwinian evolution did nothing to abate the fearful cruelties of Stalin's regime. Conversely, defenders of slavery in the antebellum American South relied heavily on scripture to justify their position. No one suggests that the Bible "causes" slavery.

Another factor contributing to the resistance to evolution is lack of understanding. "Evolution is only a theory," say those who are predisposed to reject it. In science, however, *theory* is a word reserved for a well-established, evidence-backed explanation for a body of facts. To be sure, science does not claim absolute certainty. All theories are provisional, that is, subject to change as new knowledge comes to light. Still, a theory is vastly more reliable than a hypothesis, which is formulated at an early stage of scientific inquiry.

Another misunderstanding arises from the role of chance in evolution. The late British astronomer Fred Hoyle famously expressed his disdain for evolution by likening it to a whirlwind racing through a junkyard. "What is the chance that after its passage a fully assembled 747, ready to fly, will be found standing there?"[22] he asked.

Evolutionists retort that this question grossly misrepresents the theory. Chance is only one component of evolution, they point out, limited to creating genetic variation. Selection is anything but random. Zoologist Richard Dawkins, in a rebuke to Hoyle, writes: "Our answer . . . is that natural selection is *cumulative*. There is a ratchet, such that small gains are saved. The hurricane doesn't spontaneously assemble the airliner in one go. Small improvements are added bit by bit."[23]

Evolution's Attraction

As Dawkins illustrates, most scientists go out of their way to defend evolution, and this defense in turn provokes intense criticism. Some critics charge that evolution has become an "atheist religion" and that scientists such as Dawkins are defenders of the faith. Such charges ignore the fact that many evolutionary biologists are adherents of conventional religions. Kenneth R. Miller is a practicing Catholic. Francis Collins, an evolutionary scientist who headed the U.S. government's Human Genome Project, says, "I'd call myself a serious Christian."[24]

He and other biologists accept evolution because it has proven to be a highly successful theory. According to the National Academy of Sciences (NAS), evolution alone answers the fundamental question in biology: What accounts for the staggering diversity and equally astounding relatedness of all life?[25] Darwin's theory answers this question by asserting that all life descends from a common ancestor (thus all life shares, at a minimum, DNA), and that life forms adapt to their environments through variation and natural selection over time (thus explaining diversity).

Still, an explanation, however persuasive, cannot be scientific unless evidence can be found to support it. One of the chief reasons why evolution commands nearly unanimous support among scientists in the relevant fields is that *multiple* lines of evidence support evolution.

Most famous is the fossil record. In Darwin's time this was indeed a spotty text. Since then, however, paleontologists have made enormous progress in filling in the gaps. In the view of the NAS the record, while still imperfect and sometimes hard to interpret, is convincing:

> So many intermediate forms have been discovered between fish and amphibians, between amphibians and reptiles, between reptiles and mammals, and along the primate lines of descent that it often is difficult to identify categorically when the transition occurs from one to another particular species. . . . The fossil record thus provides consistent evidence of systematic change through time—of descent with modification. From this huge body of evidence, it can be predicted that no reversals will be found in future paleontological studies. That is, amphibians will not appear before fishes, nor mammals before reptiles, and no complex life will occur in the geological record before the oldest eucaryotic cells. This prediction has been upheld by the evidence that has accumulated until now: no reversals have been found.[26]

The point about prediction should be noted, for it is characteristic of scientific theories that they yield falsifiable predictions. If reliable evidence of humans living in the dinosaur age were to be found, it would, in Dawkins' words, "blow the theory of evolution out of the water."[27] However, despite some claims to the contrary, no such evidence has been discovered.

Other Lines of Evidence

To many biologists the fossil record is secondary. They view life itself as the primary evidence for evolution. One line noted by Darwin himself is homology—common structures adapted to differing tasks in different organisms. A vivid example of homology is the hand. Birds and bats both fly, but the structure of a bat's wing is vastly more similar to a human hand or a dolphin's fin than to a bird's wing. From this (and other commonalties), biologists deduce that humans, bats, and dolphins share a more recent common ancestor with each other than they do with birds. Homology is not always easy to distinguish; sometimes the challenge of a particular environment results in distantly related organisms developing the same feature. (This is known as convergent evolution.) Nevertheless, biologists consider homology one of the key lines of evidence for evolution.

Vestigial, or leftover, organs provide especially strong evidence for Darwin's theory. The wings of an ostrich and the tailbone of humans (structures no longer used) are examples of features that biologists regard as strong evidence of ongoing evolution. As one paper on the subject puts it, "In the absence of evolutionary theory, there is no reason for wings to exist on flightless species or eyes to exist on blind species."[28]

Finally, evolution, though invisible in daily life, has been observed. The most celebrated observations took place on the Galápagos Islands, where Darwin himself collected species that eventually inspired his theory. Beginning in the 1970s, teams of biologists led by Peter and Rosemary Grant conducted exquisitely precise measurements of finches on one of the islands. In the span of a few years their data revealed natural selection at work. A persistent drought forced the finches to compete for survival, and selection rewarded those with large beaks (best suited to crack the dwindling supply of hard seeds) with survival until the mating season. In the next generation the large beak was measurably more prevalent in the population. A few years later, when heavy rains came, different adaptations resulted.[29] Their data surprised many scientists, who had thought that evolution worked too slowly to be recorded in "real time."

Creationist critics, however, are unimpressed with the Grants' work because no new species were observed by them. Carl Wieland scoffed, "After all the 'hype' about watching 'evolution', one reads with amazement that the selection events observed actually turned out to have no net long-term effect."[30]

Enduring Conflict

Of course, questions remain about evolution even for the most ardent evolutionist. All the same, scientific confidence in the theory has never been stronger. In 2002 the American Association for the Advancement of Science affirmed: "The contemporary theory of biological evolution is one of the most robust products of scientific inquiry. It is the foundation for research in many areas of biology as well as an essential element of science education."[31]

By the same token the determination of its detractors has never wavered. During a five-year stretch from 1999 to 2004, creationists lobbied for changes in education standards in Kansas, Nebraska, and Ohio, as well as in traditional bastions of antievolution sentiment such as Louisiana in the hope of removing evolution from the curriculum. In support of intelligent design, CSC published a list of one hundred scientists who doubted evolution. In response the NCSE launched "Project Steve," a list of scientists with the first name Steve (representing about 1 percent of all scientists) who endorsed evolution. The list soon topped two hundred names.

It is impossible to predict the course of public policy concerning evolution, but one thing is certain: The consequences are no longer academic. Evolution has advanced from theory to practice. Its principles are being employed in medicine, psychology, and computer science, among other fields. Its synthesis with genetics has given rise to biotechnology, which in turn has made it possible to transfer traits from one species to another. For example, bacterial genes have been inserted into the genomes of crops to make them insect resistant. But insects, in turn, have begun to evolve resistance to the toxins in transgenic crops. In view of the central role that evolution plays in so many important fields of research, treatment, and innovation, it seems likely that, no matter what public opinion is on the theory, the majority of scientists will agree with the late geneticist Theodosius Dobzhansky, who said, "Nothing in biology makes sense except in the light of evolution."[32]

Notes

1. Charles Darwin, *On the Origin of Species by Means of Natural Selection*. London: John Murray, 1859, p. 127.

2. Quoted in Francis Darwin, *The Life and Letters of Charles Darwin*, vol. 1. New York: Appleton, 1904, p. 535.

3. Samuel Wilberforce, *Essays Contributed to the* Quarterly Review, vol. 1. London: 1874, p. 95.

4. Louis Agassiz, "Evolution and Permanence of Type," *Atlantic Monthly*, 1874.

5. Agassiz, "Evolution and Permanence of Type."

6. Ronald L. Numbers, *The Creationists*. New York: Alfred A. Knopf, 1992, p. ix.

7. Asa Gray, review of *On the Origin of Species by Means of Natural Selection*, *American Journal of Science and Arts*, March 1860.

8. Thomas Huxley, "A Letter to Darwin," November 23, 1859. http://aleph0. clarku.edu/huxley/letters/59.html#23nov1859.

9. Quoted in "Thomas Henry Huxley (1825–1895)," University of California Museum of Paleontology. www.ucmp.berkeley.edu/history/thuxley. html.

10. Charles Darwin, "Letter to Huxley," November 25, 1859. http://charles-darwin.classic-literature.co.uk/the-life-and-letters-of-charles-darwin-volume-ii/ebook-page-14.asp.

11. Numbers, *The Creationists*, p. 73.

12. Numbers, *The Creationists*, p. 209.

13. *Epperson v. Arkansas*, 393 U.S. 97 (1968).

14. *Edwards v. Aguillard*, 482 U.S. 578 (1987).

15. Center for Science and Culture, "Top Questions." www.discovery.org/csc/topQuestions.php.

16. Talkdesign.org, "Do Scientists Support Intelligent Design?" www.talk design.org/introfaq.html.

17. Richard Monastersky, "Society Disowns Paper Attacking Darwinism," *Chronicle of Higher Education*, September 24, 2004.

18. Kenneth R. Miller, "The Flaw in the Mousetrap," *Natural History*, April 2002.

19. Phillip E. Johnson, "Creator or Blind Watchmaker?" *First Things*, 1993.

20. Deborah Jordan Brooks, "Substantial Numbers of Americans Continue to Doubt Evolution as Explanation for Origin of Humans," Gallup News Service, March 5, 2001. www.unl.edu.

21. Don Boys, "Evolution Is a Farce, a Fraud, a Fake and a Faith!" Cornerstone Communications, 2000. www.cstnews.com.

22. Fred Hoyle, *The Intelligent Universe*. London: Michael Joseph, 1983, p. 19.

23. Richard Dawkins, "Human Chauvinism," *Evolution*, vol. 51, no. 3, June 1997.

24. Quoted in PBS, *Religion and Ethics Newsweekly.* www.pbs.org/wnet/religionandethics/transcripts/collins.html.

25. National Academies Press, *Teaching About Evolution and the Nature of Science*, 1998. www.nap.edu/readingroom/books/evolution98/evol1.html.

26. National Academies Press, *Science and Creationism: A View from the National Academy of Sciences.* http://books.nap.edu/html/creationism/evidence.html.

27. Richard Dawkins, "Sadly, an Honest Creationist," *Free Inquiry*, Fall 2001.

28. Reed A. Cartwright and Douglas L. Theobald, "Citing Scadding (1981) and Misunderstanding Vestigiality," Talk.Origins Archive, December 8, 2003. www.talkorigins.org/faqs/quotes/scadding.html.

29. Quoted in Jonathan Weiner, *The Beak of the Finch: A Story of Evolution in Our Time.* New York: Vintage, 1995, pp. 146–48.

30. Carl Wieland, "The Beak of the Finch: Evolution in Real Time," *Creation*, 1995.

31. American Association for the Advancement of Science, "AAAS Board Resolution on Intelligent Design Theory." www.aaas.org/news/releases/2002/1106id2.shtml.

32. Theodosius Dobzhansky, "Nothing in Biology Makes Sense Except in Light of Evolution," *American Biology Teacher*, March 1973, p. 125.

CHAPTER 1

Origins of
a Theory

Ancient Greek Speculations on the Origins of Life

By G.E.R. Lloyd

Ancient peoples generally believed that supernatural forces lay behind natural phenomena. However, among the Greeks in the fifth century B.C., some philosophers began to seek natural explanations. As G.E.R. Lloyd relates in the following selection, these early scientists had little more than observation, reason, and speculation to work with, yet they drew some remarkably astute conclusions. To counter supernatural claims about lightning, for example, Greek philosopher Anaximander proposed that lightning occurs when clouds split apart. He also considered the origins of life, arguing that some animals, in particular humans, must have evolved from others. Later, Aristotle advanced his own theories of life. A keen observer, Aristotle contributed much to the ancient study of biology, including a theory that offspring inherit characteristics from their parents. However, contrary to the modern theory of evolution, he believed that animals remain fixed within their own kind, rather than giving rise to new species. G.E.R. Lloyd is Emeritus Professor of Ancient Philosophy and Science at the University of Cambridge.

I t is clear that the Milesians [philosophers of Miletus] paid a good deal of attention to rare or striking natural phenomena. If we ask why this was so, part of the answer may lie in their desire to provide naturalistic explanations for phenomena that were usually considered to be controlled by the gods. Zeus was responsible for the thunderbolt and Poseidon for earthquakes, and Atlas held the earth up on his shoulders. The bid to give naturalistic explanations was going to be judged especially by its success or failure to account for events that were popularly believed to be produced by supernatural agencies. Thus [philosopher and scientist] Thales . . . explained earthquakes as occurring when the earth is rocked on the water on which it floats. Similarly Anaximander [a student of Thales] suggested that thunderbolts are cause by wind and that lightning is produced when clouds are split in two. Naïve as these explanations are, their significance lies not so much in what they include as in what they omit, that is the arbitrary wills and quasi-human motivation of the anthropomorphic gods.

Moreover in some cases the Milesians went far beyond merely countering popular beliefs in the supernatural. Two examples from Anaximander are particularly interesting. First he attempted an account of the heavenly bodies, picturing them as rings of fire. The rings themselves cannot be seen since they are surrounded by mist, but they have openings through which the heavenly bodies appear: what we see as a star is like a puncture in a vast celestial bicycle wheel. He postulated three such rings for the sun, the moon and the stars: the diameters of the rings are twenty-seven, eighteen and nine times the diameter of the earth, the earth iself being represented as a flat-topped cylinder, three times as broad as it is deep, at rest at the centre of the rings, and he suggested that eclipses of the sun and moon occur when the apertures through which they are seen become blocked. Many difficulties remain: how the circle or sphere of the fixed stars is conceived is far from clear; nothing is said about the planets as such; most strangely, the fixed stars are held to be below both the sun and the moon. Nevertheless the importance of this theory is that it is the first attempt at what we may term a mechanical model of the heavenly bodies in Greek astronomy.

A Rough Sketch of Evolution

My second example is the theory Anaximander proposed concerning the origin of animals in general and of man in particular. This too was a topic on which several myths were current in ancient Greece. There was the story of Deucalion and Pyrrha, for example, who, when the flood had wiped out the human race, created more men and women by throwing stones over their shoulders. In other stories mankind was represented as related to and derived from the gods. As we should expect, Anaximander's approach to this subject is quite different. According to a report in the third-century A.D. doxographer Hippolytus, he held that living creatures are first generated in the 'wet' when this is acted on by the sun. No doubt, like most Greeks, he believed that animals may be spontaneously generated in certain substances under certain conditions, and this idea provided the basis for an account of the origin of animals as a whole. But he also suggested that man was originally born in a different species of animal, that is, apparently, some sort of fish. Another of our sources, Plutarch, refers in this context to the *galeoi* or dog-fish, one species of which, the so-called 'smooth shark', is remarkable in that the young are attached by a navel-string to a placenta-like formation in the womb of the female parent. Many scholars have considered it unlikely that Anaximander himself knew of that particular species, but if Plutarch's report has any substance at all, it can hardly be doubted that Anaximander had some knowledge of viviparous sea-animals of some sort.

Human Origins

But the question of what empirical basis, if any, Anaximander's theory may have had is less important than the reasoning that led him to propose it in the first place. The original stimulus seems to have been the observation that on birth the human infant takes a long time to become self-sufficient. Anaximander seems to have appreciated that this created a serious difficulty for anyone who supposed that the human race originated with the sudden appearance, on earth, of the young of the human species. He preferred to argue that humans must originally have been born from a different species of animal which was able to nurture them long enough for them to become self-sufficient. Neither Anaximander nor any other Greek theorist developed a systematic theory of the evolution of natural species as a whole. But as this example shows, the Greek philosophers began at an early stage to reflect on the problems posed by the origin of the human race and by man's development from nature to culture. . . .

Aristotle's View

The branch of natural science that received most attention from Aristotle is biology—the biological treatises make up more than a fifth of his total extant work—and the reason for this is clear.

Living creatures and their parts provided far more evidence of the roles of form and the final cause than inanimate objects did. . . . He felt the need to justify the study of animals and was conscious of being a pioneer in this field. Against the Platonists and all who disparaged the use of observation, he insisted on the value and importance of detailed research in biology. Anyone who is willing to take sufficient trouble can learn a great deal concerning each one of the different kinds of animals and plants, and 'to the intellect the craftsmanship of nature provides extraordinary pleasures for those who can recognise the causes in things'.

The range of his zoological researches is remarkable. Well over 500 different species of animals, including about 120 kinds of fish and sixty kinds of insects, are referred to in the biological works. His data were collected from a wide variety of sources: he relied a good deal on fishermen, hunters, horse-trainers, bee-keepers and the like, but also undertook his own personal researches. In some cases we can infer with some probability when and where his work was carried out. The biological treatises contain some particularly detailed accounts of the marine animals in the Lagoon of Pyrrha on Lesbos and we know that Aristotle spent a couple of years (344–342 [B.C.]) on that island. While he was certainly not the first biologist to use the method of dissection, he was the first to do so extensively. It is impossible to give a precise estimate of the number of species he dissected, and they evidently did not include man: in the *Inquiry Concerning Animals* he remarks that 'the inner parts of man are for the most part unknown, and so we must refer to the parts of other animals which those of man resemble, and examine them'. Nevertheless our texts contain many detailed reports that give information that could only have been obtained from dissections, and numerous passages refer directly to the method. . . .

Error and Method

To be sure, the biological treatises contain, as Aristotle's critics have been quick to point out, many mistakes, some of them simple ones—as when he gives the number of teeth in women or the number of ribs in man incorrectly—others more serious, such as his belief that the brain is bloodless, and the influential doctrine associated with this, that the heart is the seat of sensation. Yet his attitude towards the evidence he collected from his informants is, in general, a cautious and critical one. He often speaks of the need to verify the data—particularly concerning rare animals or exceptional phenomena—and, when the available evidence appears to him to be inadequate, he draws attention to this fact. Two passages will illustrate this. In *On the Generation of Animals* he considers the possibility of some species of animals reproducing parthenogenetically:

> If there is any kind of animal which is female and has no separate male, it is possible that this generates offspring from itself. Up till now, at least, this has not been reliably observed, but some cases in the class of fishes make us hesitate. Thus no male of the fish called *erythrinos* has ever been seen, but females have, including females full of roe. But of this we have as yet no reliable proof. . . .

Sharp Observer

Some of the discoveries that Aristotle made or recorded are justly famous. One of the most remarkable is his account of a species of dog-fish, the so-called 'smooth shark'. . . . The species in question, *Mustelus laevis*, is externally viviparous, as indeed are several of the cartilaginous fishes, but it is exceptional in that the embryo is attached by a navel-string to a placenta-like structure in the womb of the female parent. Aristotle's description in the *Inquiry Concerning Animals* is clear and precise, yet it was generally disbelieved until Johannes Müller published the results of his investigations of this and related species in 1842—investigations which largely vindicated the accuracy of Aristotle's account. And it is not only for the discovery of such exceptional phenomena as this that Aristotle has won praise from naturalists, but also for his meticulous descriptions of the external and internal parts of such familiar species as the crawfish.

Aristotle demonstrates his skill as an observer in passage after passage in the biological treatises. But his chief motive for studying animals was, as we have seen, not description, but explanation, to establish the causes at work and especially the formal and final causes. The work *On the Parts of Animals* deals mainly with the causes of the various parts of the body, and in *On the Generation of Animals, On the Motion of Animals, On the Progression of Animals* and the short treatises known as the *Parva Naturalia* he also tackles a wide range of physiological problems, including nutrition and growth, respiration, locomotion and, especially, reproduction. Not surprisingly, the positive conclusions that he reached on these obscure questions are usually wide of the mark. Nevertheless his discussions have at least two considerable merits; first, in the clarity with which the problems themselves are formulated, and secondly, in the ingenuity and acuteness with which he develops and analyses the arguments on either side.

An Analysis of Inheritance

One example which will illustrate this is his discussion of one of the fundamental problems of reproduction, the question of whether the seed is drawn from the whole of the parent's body or not. The view that it is, the 'pangenesis' theory, had been advocated by the atomists and by some of the medical writers, but is severely criticised by Aristotle. In *On the Generation of Animals* he sets out the problem and cites the main evidence and arguments that had been used to support pangenesis. So far as the evidence goes, he questions or flatly denies its validity. Thus it had commonly been supposed that not only congenital but also acquired characteristics—Aristotle's terms are *symphytos* and *epiktetos*—are inherited, and that mutilated parents, for example, have mutilated offspring. But to this Aristotle replied by simply denying that this is always the case.

Against pangenesis he brings some ingenious and telling counter-arguments. One aims to show that the theory is incoherent by posing a dilemma. The seed must be drawn either (*i*) from all the uniform parts—Aristotle means flesh, bone, sinew and so on—or (*ii*) from all the non-uniform parts—by which he means the hand, the face and so on, or (*iii*) from both. But against (*i*) he objects that the resemblances that children show to their parents lie rather in such features as their faces and hands than in their flesh and bones as such. And against (*ii*) he points out that the non-uniform parts are actually composed of the uniform ones. A hand is made up of flesh, bone, blood, nail and so on. Against (*iii*) he uses the same consideration. Resemblances in the nonuniform parts must be due either to the material—but *that* is simply the uniform parts—or to the way in which the material is arranged. But if to the latter, nothing can be said to be 'drawn' from the *arrangement* to the seed, for the arrangement is not itself a material factor. In either case the seed cannot be drawn from such parts as the hands or face, but only from what those parts are made of. But then the theory loses its point, which was that all the individual parts of the body, and not merely all the constituent substances, supply material to the seed.

He rejects the pangenesis doctrine, then, and in the main he was right to do so, even though his own positive theory concerning what each parent contributes to the offspring was in certain respects very mistaken. He believed, for example, that the semen of the male contributes no material to the embryo, but merely supplies the form and the efficient cause of generation.

A second more fundamental controversy in biology concerned the role of the final cause itself. Whereas both Plato and Aristotle insisted on the element of rational design throughout nature and in living creatures in particular, other theorists, and especially Empedocles and the atomists, had generally adopted a mechanistic, non-teleological stand-point in their accounts of natural causation. The evidence about Empedocles is particularly interesting, though extremely obscure. In *On the Parts of Animals* Aristotle ascribes to him the view that

> animals have many characteristics that are the result of incidental occurrences in their formation,—for instance the backbone is as it is [divided into vertebrae] because the foetus becomes contorted and so the backbone is broken.

Natural Selection?

Again Simplicius, dealing, in his *Commentary on Aristotle's Physics*, with the famous fragment in which Empedocles spoke of the birth of 'man-headed oxen', reports that he held that

> during the rule of Love there came to be by chance first of all the parts of animals, such as heads and hands and feet, and then these 'man-headed oxen' came together, and 'conversely there sprang up' ox-headed men . . . . And as many of these as were fitted together to one another so as to ensure their preservation, became animals and survived. . . . For all that did not come together according to the proper formula (*logos*) perished.

Although there are obvious superficial similarities between these notions and the doctrine of the evolution of species, it must be remembered first, that Empedocles was not attempting a systematic account of the origin of natural species at all, and secondly, that his ideas were developed in the context of a highly fanciful cosmological doctrine of the cycle during which the two cosmic forces of Love and Strife come to rule in turn.

In arguing against those who tended to deny design in living creatures, Aristotle no doubt believed that the evidence pointed overwhelmingly in his favour. He knew, of course, that abnormalities and monstrous births do occur, but the important point, in his view, was that these were the exceptions to a rule that held good in the vast majority of instances. One of the chief considerations that he brings against Empedocles and the atomists is simply that natural species reproduce according to kind. In *On the Parts of Animals* he says that Empedocles ignored the fact that the seed which produces any animal must have the appropriate specific character of that animal. It is a man that begets a man, an ox that begets an ox: the idea that natural species themselves were the result of chance mutations would have seemed to him not only to have no direct evidence in its support, but also to fly in the face of the existing evidence of the normal circumstances of the reproduction of natural species.

A Special Place for Man

The notions of form and final cause permeate the whole of Aristotle's philosophy. They are fundamental not only to his natural science, but also to his cosmology: the primary cause on which the universe depends and from which all movement is ultimately derived is an Unmoved Mover which is said to bring about movement as final cause, as the good that is the object of desire and love. Form and finality are equally prominent in his ethics and politics too, for his ideas of the good life, and of the good state, are based on his conception of man's proper ends or function. Man has a unique place on the scale of being: he shares with the gods the possession of reason, but with the other animals the possession of his other vital faculties, such as sensation, nutrition and reproduction. At the same time it is a *single* scale of being that comprehends gods, men, animals, plants and inanimate objects. Different natural objects have different forms and ends, but every kind of natural object from the divine heavenly bodies down to the humblest pebble seeks and aspires to the form and end appropriate to it.

The Other Darwin

By Erasmus Darwin

Erasmus Darwin died seven years before Charles Darwin was born, yet he had an enormous influence on his famous grandson. In his book *Zoonomia*, the senior Darwin outlines many ideas that would be crucial to his grandson's theory of evolution. In this excerpt from *Zoonomia*, he infers a single common ancestor for all animals. He proposes that species emerged over immense periods of time, an idea central to his grandson's theory of evolution and contrary to the six-day creation story so widely accepted in his time. Darwin also cites the similar body plans of a great many animals as evidence of common ancestry. This idea, later to become known as homology, would become a key argument for evolution. He concludes this passage by suggesting that it would be a greater feat for the Almighty to achieve biological diversity by the indirect processes suggested in *Zoonomia* than by direct creation. A true intellectual, Erasmus Darwin was known in his time not only as a respected physician but also as a poet, philosopher, botanist, and naturalist.

All animals have a similar origin, viz. from a single living filament; and that the difference of their forms and qualities has arisen only from the different irritabilities and sensibilities, or voluntarities, or associabilities, of this original living filament; and perhaps in some degree from the different forms of the particles of the fluids, by which it has been first stimulated into activity. And that from hence, as [Carl] Linnæus [founder of biological classification] has conjectured in respect to the vegetable world, it is not impossible, but the great variety of species of animals, which now tenant the earth, may have had their origin from the mixture of a few natural orders. And that those animal and vegetable mules [hybrids], which could continue their species, have done so, and constitute the numerous families of animals and vegetables which now exist; and that those mules, which were pro-

Erasmus Darwin, *Zoonomia; or, the Laws of Organic Life, Volume 1*. Boston: Thomas and Andrews, 1803.

duced with imperfect organs of generation, perished without reproduction, according to the observation of Aristotle; and are the
animals, which we now call mules. . . .

Such a promiscuous intercourse of animals is said to exist at this
day in New South Wales [Australia] by [British naval] Captain
[John] Hunter. And that not only amongst the quadrupeds and birds
of different kinds, but even amongst the fish, and, as he believes,
amongst the vegetables. He speaks of an animal between the opossum and the kangaroo, from the size of a sheep to that of a rat. . . .

All animals therefore, I contend, have a similar cause of their organization, originating from a single living filament, endued indeed
with different kinds of irritabilities and sensibilities, or of animal
appetencies; which exist in every gland, and in every moving organ
of the body, and are as essential to living organization as chemical
affinities are to certain combinations of inanimate matter.

If I might be indulged to make a simile in a philosophical work,
I should say, that the animal appetencies, are not only perhaps less
numerous originally than the chemical affinities; but that like these
latter, they change with every new combination; thus vital air and
azote, when combined, produce nitrous acid; which now acquires
the property of dissolving silver; so with every new additional part
to the embryon, as of the throat or lungs, I suppose a new animal
appetency to be produced. . . .

When we revolve in our minds, first, the great changes, which
we see naturally produced in animals after their nativity, as in the
production of the butterfly with painted wings from the crawling
caterpillar; or of the respiring frog from the subnatant tadpole;
from the feminine boy to the bearded man, and from the infant girl
to the lactescent woman; both which changes may be prevented
by certain mutilations of the glands necessary to reproduction.

The Role of Breeding

Secondly, when we think over the great changes introduced into
various animals by artificial or accidental cultivation, as in horses,
which we have exercised for the different purposes of strength or
swiftness, in carrying burthens or in running races; or in dogs,
which have been cultivated for strength and courage, as the bulldog; or for acuteness of his sense of smell, as the hound and
spaniel; or for the swiftness of his foot, as the greyhound; or for
his swimming in the water, or for drawing snow sledges, as the

rough-haired dogs of the north; or lastly, as a play-dog for children, as the lap-dog; with the changes of the forms of the cattle, which have been domesticated from the greatest antiquity, as camels, and sheep; which have undergone so total a transformation, that we are now ignorant from what species of wild animals they had their origin. . . .

Thirdly, when we enumerate the great changes produced in the species of animals before their nativity; these are such as resemble the form or colour of their parents, which have been altered by the cultivation or accidents above related, and are thus continued to their posterity. Or they are changes produced by the mixture of species as in mules; or changes produced probably by the exuberance of nourishment suppled to the fetus, as in monstrous births with additional limbs; many of these enormities of shape are propagated, and continued as a variety at least, if not as a new species of animal. I have seen a breed of cats with an additional claw on every foot; of poultry also with an additional claw, and with wings to their feet; and of others without rumps. . . . There are many kinds of pigeons admired for their peculiarities, which are monsters thus produced and propagated. And to these must be added, the changes produced by the imagination of the male parent. . . .

When we consider all these changes of animal form, and innumerable others, which may be collected from the books of natural history; we cannot but be convinced, that the fetus or embryon is formed by apposition of new parts, and not by the differentiation of a primordial nest of germes [germs], included one within another, like the cups of a conjurer.

Structural Similarities

Fourthly, when we revolve in our minds the great similarity of structure which obtains in all the warm-blooded animals, as well quadrupeds, birds, and amphibious animals, as in mankind; from the mouse and bat to the elephant and whale; one is led to conclude, that they have alike been produced from a similar living filament. In some this filament in its advance to maturity has acquired hands and fingers, with a fine sense of touch, as in mankind. In others it has acquired claws or talons, as in tygers and eagles. In others, toes with an intervening web, or membrane, as in seals and geese. In others it has acquired cloven hoofs, as in cows and swine; and whole hoofs in others, as in the horse. While in the bird kind this original living filament has put forth wings instead of arms and legs, and feathers instead of hair. In some it has protruded horns on the forehead instead of teeth in the fore part of the upper jaw; in others tushes instead of horns; in others beaks instead of either. And all this exactly as is daily seen in the transmutations of the tadpole, which acquires legs and lungs, when he wants them; and loses his tail, when it is no longer of service to him. . . .

The contrivances for the purposes of security extend even to vegetables, as is seen in the wonderful and various means of their concealing or defending their honey from insects, and their seeds from birds. On the other hand swiftness of wing has been acquired by hawks and swallows to pursue their prey; and a proboscis of admirable structure has been acquired by the bee, the moth, and the humming bird, for the purpose of plundering the nectaries of flowers. All which seem to have been formed by the original living filament, excited into action by the necessities of the creatures, which possess them, and on which their existence depends.

Taking the Long View

From thus meditating on the great similarity of the structure of the warm-blooded animals, and at the same time of the great changes they undergo both before and after their nativity; and by considering in how minute a portion of time many of the changes of animals above described have been produced; would it be too bold to imagine, that in the great length of time, since the earth began to exist, perhaps millions of ages before the commencement of the history of mankind, would it be too bold to imagine, that all warm-blooded animals have arisen from one living filament, which THE GREAT FIRST CAUSE endued with animality, with the power of acquiring new parts attended with new propensities, directed by irritations, sensations, volitions, and associations; and thus possessing the faculty of continuing to improve by its own inherent activity, and of delivering down those improvements by generation to its posterity, world without end?

Sixthly, the cold-blooded animals, as the fish-tribes, which are furnished with but one ventricle of the heart, and with gills instead of lungs, and with fins instead of feet or wings, bear a great similarity to each other; but they differ, nevertheless, so much in their general structure from warm-blooded animals, that it may not seem probable at first view, that the same living filament could have given origin to this kingdom of animals, as to the former. Yet are there some creatures, which unite or partake of both these orders of animation, as the whales and seals; and more particularly the frog, who changes from an aquatic animal furnished with gills to an aerial one furnished with lungs. . . .

Linnæus supposes, in the introduction to his *Natural Orders*, that very few vegetables were at first created, and that their numbers were increased by their intermarriages. . . . [He notes that] many other changes seem to have arisen in them by their perpetual contest for light and air above ground, and for food or moisture beneath the soil. . . . Other changes of vegetables from climate, or other causes, are remarked in the Note on Curcuma in the same work. From these one might be led to imagine, that each plant at first consisted of a single bulb or flower to each root, as the gentianella and daisy; and that in the contest for air and light new buds grew on the old decaying flower stem, shooting down their elongated roots to the ground, and that in process of ages tall trees were thus formed, and an individual bulb became a swarm of vegetables. Other plants, which in this contest for light and air were too slender to rise by their own strength, learned by degrees to adhere to their neighbors, either by putting forth roots like the ivy, or by tendrils like the vine, or by spiral contortions like the honey-suckle; or by growing upon them like the misleto, and taking nourishment from their barks; or by lodging or adhering on them, and deriving nourishment from the air, as tillandsia.

Plants Before Animals

Shall we then say that the vegetable living filament was originally different from that of each tribe of animals above described? And that the productive living filament of each of those tribes was different originally from the other? Or, as the earth and ocean were probably peopled with vegetable productions long before the existence of animals; and many families of these animals long before other families of them, shall we conjecture that one and the same kind of living filament is and has been the cause of all organic life?

If this gradual production of the species and genera of animals be assented to, a contrary circumstance may be supposed to have occurred, namely, that some kinds by the great changes of the elements may have been destroyed. This idea is shewn [shown] to our senses by contemplating the petrifactions of shells, and of vegetables, which may be said, like busts and medals, to record the history of remote times. Of the myriads of belemnites, cornua ammonis, and numerous other petrified shells, which are found in the masses of lime-stone, which have been produced by them, none now are ever found in our seas, or in the seas of other parts of the world, according to the observations of many naturalists. Some of whom have imagined, that most of the inhabitants of the sea and earth of very remote times are now extinct; as they scarcely admit, that a single fossil shell bears a strict similitude to any recent ones, and that the vegetable impressions or petrifactions found in iron-ores, clay, or sandstone, of which there are many of the fern kind, are not similar to any plants of this country, nor accurately correspond with those of other climates, which is an argument countenancing the changes in the forms, both of animals and vegetables, during the progressive structure of the globe, which we inhabit. . . .

This idea of the gradual formation and improvement of the animal world accords with the observations of some modern philosophers, who have supposed that the continent of America has been raised out of the ocean at a later period of time than the other three quarters of the globe, which they deduce from the greater comparative heights of its mountains, and the consequent greater coldness of its respective climates, and from the less size and strength of its animals, as the tygers and allegators compared with those of Asia and Africa. And lastly, from the less progress in the improvements of the mind of its inhabitants in respect to voluntary exertions.

Earlier Opinions

This idea of the gradual formation and improvement of the animal world seems not to have been unknown to the ancient philosophers. Plato having probably observed the reciprocal generation of inferior animals, as snails and worms, was of opinion, that mankind with all other animals were originally hermaphrodites during the infancy of the world, and were in process of time separated into male and female. . . .

The late [Scottish philospher] Mr. David Hume, in his posthumous works, places the powers of generation much above those of our boasted reason; and adds, that reason can only make a machine, as a clock or a ship, but the power of generation makes the maker of the machine; and probably from having observed, that the greatest part of the earth has been formed out of organic recrements; as the immense beds of limestone, chalk, marble, from the shells of fish; and the extensive provinces of clay, sandstone, ironstone, coals, from decomposed vegetables; all which have been first produced by generation, or by the secretions or organic life; he concludes that the world itself might have been generated, rather than created; that is, it might have been gradually produced from very small beginnings, increasing by the activity of its inherent principles, rather than by a sudden evolution of the whole by Almighty fiat.—What a magnificent idea of the infinite power of THE GREAT ARCHITECT! THE CAUSE OF CAUSES! PARENT OF PARENTS! ENS ENTIUM [the being of all beings]!

For if we may compare infinities, it would seem to require a greater infinity of power to cause the causes of effects, than to cause the effects themselves. This idea is analogous to the improving excellence observable in every part of the creation; such as in the progressive increase of the solid or habitable parts of the earth from water; and in the progressive increase of the wisdom and happiness of its inhabitants; and is consonant to the idea of our present situation being a state of probation, which by our exertions we may improve, and are consequently responsible for our actions.

Lamarck Makes a False Start

By Michael Ruse

According to Michael Ruse in the following selection, at the end of the eighteenth century, French biologist Jean Baptiste de Lamarck challenged the prevailing idea that all species were fixed and unchanging. Examining fossil records, Lamarck, a contemporary of Charles Darwin, concluded that as their environments changed, animals changed in order to survive. Lamarck believed in the "chain of being" theory, which stipulates that over time animals make a fairly constant progression up the scale from simpler life-forms to more complex forms. Michael Ruse is a philosopher of science best known for his work on evolution. After a distinguished career at the University of Guelph in Ontario, Canada, he now holds an endowed chair as Lucyle T. Werkmeister Professor of Philosophy at Florida State University.

Relaxing the old way of seeing things was not an easy or straightforward matter. To us, for instance, fossils obviously imply that the earth is of great age. But this is obvious only because we see fossils as the remains of long-dead organisms. . . .

The grip of the Bible also proved very tight. It may have loosened a little toward the end of the seventeenth century, but in Britain, particularly, it clamped down hard again in the eighteenth, a direct result of the evangelicalism sparked by John Wesley [the founder of Methodism]. The Bible remained a major factor in the nineteenth century.

Nevertheless, by the end of the eighteenth century and the beginning of the nineteenth, speculation on organic evolution, though not commonplace or in any way acceptable, was no longer particularly novel. One of the best-known theories . . . was that of

Charles Darwin's grandfather, Erasmus Darwin. But undoubtedly all previous speculations paled beside the systematic evolutionary attack on the organic origins question made by the French biologist Jean Baptiste de Lamarck.

An Older Innovator

[Philosopher of science] Thomas Kuhn has remarked perceptively that the scientist who makes a really innovative move, breaking with the past and opening up new and fertile fields of scientific exploration, tends to be fairly young. This is not fortuitous: the innovative scientist must grasp the essentials of past scientific achievements while sensing acutely the problems that flaw them; but he must not be emotionally and intellectually committed to the past—for example, through having himself made significant contributions to established theories. Obviously a younger man is more likely to fit this category, and when we come to consider Charles Darwin and his work we shall find that he is the exemplar both of this pattern and of its rationale.

Lamarck, however, is something of an exception. Although in becoming an evolutionist he was not greatly innovative, and although his evolutionism contained elements drawn from his predecessors, Lamarck's conversion to evolutionism was apparently neither a phenomenon of his youth nor a drawn-out process with early beginnings, but an event that came somewhat abruptly in his fifty-sixth year. Until virtually the end of the eighteenth century, Lamarck agreed with almost everyone else that organisms and their groupings remain essentially unchanged from their first appearance. Then between 1799 and 1800 he suddenly swung to a diametrically opposite position, arguing that organisms evolve and that this evolution is constantly refueled by new organisms as life is spontaneously generated out of inorganic matter.

We do not have a wealth of material helping us reconstruct Lamarck's route to discovery or conversion. But clever detective work by a recent scholar makes it fairly clear that invertebrate taxonomy was chiefly responsible for the path Lamarck took. In 1793 Lamarck was appointed to the Museum of Natural History in Paris as professor of "insects, worms, and microscopic animals." It was a good time to be a professor at this museum, for during that decade the collections were being drastically augmented both through scientific expeditions of discovery and through the rape of other museums in Europe, as French scientists spread their tentacles in the wake of their conquering armies. And thus, given his allotted subject and the necessary means, it fell to Lamarck to try to answer the question of growing interest and importance within the scientific community: Did species of organisms always survive indefinitely, or, as had been recently claimed on the basis of comparison between living and fossil forms, did some species finally become extinct? Lamarck was in a peculiarly favored position to answer this question, because the museum's large collection of shells gave him the perfect opportunity to explore whether fossil shells always had living counterparts.

Speculation on Evolution

It seems that from his studies Lamarck was indeed compelled to admit that they did not. Yet he was unwilling to agree with many of his contemporaries that this proved the reality of total annihilation. In earlier years, particularly in Britain, people had rejected extinction because they feared it was irreligious: an extinct organism, particularly one that died out before man, seemed a blot on God's good sense. Lamarck, however, opposed extinction for almost the opposite reason. Other than by appealing to a supernatural cause, something he as a scientist was loathe to do, he could not see how may species could become extinct (except, he came to concede, in the special circumstance where man destroyed all its members). Shellfish particularly, Lamarck thought, protected in their watery homes, could not be depleted to the point of extinction. Hence, since some kinds of shellfish apparently no longer exist, evolution into other forms of life seemed the only solution. Curiously, for the very simplest forms of life Lamarck somewhat reversed himself. In their case he could not see how anything so fragile could endure all the harshness of nature: snow, frost, and so forth. Hence he felt that extinction would almost be expected; but since the simplest forms of life so obviously do not become extinct, he felt compelled to postulate the spontaneous generation of new life forms.

At the beginning of the nineteenth century, therefore, Lamarck became an evolutionist, and over the years he presented his ideas in various forms. But, partly because his ideas did not really change much and partly because this was the version best known to the British, I shall concentrate exclusively on Lamarck's ideas as given in 1809 in his *Philosophie zoologique*. Since this work has been translated, for convenience I shall refer both to the original and to the translation (in brackets).

The backbone of Lamarck's theory was the "chain of being" or "scale of nature". Lamarck believed, with reservations, that all animals can be ranged on an ascending scale, with the lowest, infusorians, at one end, and the most complex and perfect, man, at the other end. (Lamarck believed in two separate chains of being, one for animals and one for plants. Later he divided his animal chain in two.) This idea of a scale was not peculiar to Lamarck. Indeed, it has antecedents in the Platonic dialogues, perhaps proving, to extend [philosopher Alfred North] Whitehead's aphorism, that the evolutionary debate, like philosophy, is just a set of footnotes to Plato. Lamarck differed from his predecessors in that for him the scale of nature was dynamic rather than static; and this, in the broad sense in which we are using the term, made him an evolutionist. He believed that organisms made a fairly constant progression up the scale as they changed in the course of many generations from the simplest to the most complex. New primitive organisms constantly appear at the bottom of the scale as they are formed from inorganic matter.

Searching for Cause and Effect

Lamarck tried hard to be a good materialist; he denied that life or mind involved special entities or modes of understanding radically different from the inorganic world. What drove organisms up the chain of being was, first, that they experience certain needs brought about by the constantly changing environment. Then in some way, perhaps involving new habits, these trigger the movement of various bodily fluids that create or enlarge organs. These fluids are not sensible, like water or blood, but are "subtle" fluids like electricity and caloric. In the higher animals, between the needs and the fluids, Lamarck sandwiched his famous—or perhaps notorious—inner consciousness, which acts as a causal link enabling the organism to respond physiologically to its needs. Although all his critics later accused Lamarck of postulating consciousness in animals that obviously cannot really think, it seems clear that the *sentiment intérieur* did not involve true thought but was a kind of "life force."

Despite his materialist intention, however, matters were not quite as straightforward as they first appear. Sometimes Lamarck wrote as though everything happens in the normal causal manner, just as in physics. An environmental change occurs, a need is set up, and so on. When critics claimed that evolution was impossible because animals mummified by the ancient Egyptians are identical to today's animals, he retorted that there had been no environmental change in Egypt since ancient times. But at other times he implied that progression up the scale of being will occur no matter what happens or fails to happen. Thus he argued that the chain of being would be perfectly regular even if all organisms were in a uniform, demand-free environment. Moreover, ignoring for the moment a secondary factor that he added to his chain-of-being doctrine, Lamarck seemed to envision an inevitable passage as organisms moved up the chain. This leads one to suspect that, materialist or no, Lamarck saw things in the organic world as being end-directed, with the end in the animal world being man. In a sense, therefore, he was a *teleologist*, trying to explain in terms of ends rather than merely prior material causes.

Inherited Experience

On this main thesis about organic change, Lamarck superimposed another evolutionary mechanism, if we can so describe it without prejudice. This mechanism seems to differ from the first primarily, if not solely, in that it is supposed to lead to anomalies, branchings, and irregularities in the chain of being—for instance, causing the birds to be put off on one side. Sometimes this secondary mechanism was said to act directly through the environment, as when poor nutrition causes stunted growth, which Lamarck thought was heritable. Sometimes it involved habits, as in change through use and disuse. Lamarck drew attention to animal and plant breeding. We find, for example, that when ducks are not allowed to fly, they lose their power of flight permanently, and this appears to be inevitable. Lamarck suggested that the same applies naturally, thus disturbing the uniform climb up the chain of being.

This, then, was Lamarck's evolutionary theory—at least as I understand it, for it must be confessed that he is the most confusing of writers. Indeed, we will learn that the conceptually fuzzy way Lamarck presented his ideas had interesting implications for our story. One suspects that Lamarck is confusing because he was confused. Certainly his secondary "mechanism" seems little more than an ad hoc device for getting around problems. But this much we can say. Lamarck accepted a chain of being with irregularities. He thought that the satisfaction of needs was a significant cause of heritable change. This inheritance of acquired variations or characteristics is what we today call "Lamarckism"—somewhat inaccurately, for it was not his whole theory, nor was it original with him. Yet I would not deny Lamarck his rightful place in history. It is one thing to have an idea for change. It is quite another to have the imagination to use it to support a full-blown evolutionary theory.

One way to make Lamarck's theory more plausible is to argue that only his second mechanism involves needs, habits, and inner consciousness. The first simply involves the body's fluids blindly carving out new paths, leading to new characteristics and thus driving organisms up the scale of nature. There is some justification for this interpretation in the *Philosophie zoologique*. . . . But, even ignoring the fact that there is no reason to think so undirected a mechanism as fluids making new channels can lead to so teleological a result as the drive up the scale of being, the *Philosophie zoologique* certainly claims that habits are involved in all permanent change. Consequently, if people see "Lamarckism" as the essence of Lamarck's theorizing, it is really nobody's fault but his own.

Troubled by Species

Lamarck's theory may have concerned the origins of organisms, but it was not a theory of the origins of species. He hoped to explain organic diversity, but species—distinct kinds of organisms, unable to breed with other kinds—were something of an embarrassment to him. Since he believed essentially in a gradual, continuous chain, he had to explain gaps between organisms by various ad hoc hypotheses—that we have not yet found the bridging organisms, that man has destroyed them, that the secondary mechanism may have caused gaps.

Also, one must note that Lamarck's theory was in no way a theory of common descent, supposing that all organisms descend from one or a few common origins. We know that he thought simple forms of life are constantly being spontaneously generated through the action of heat, light, electricity, and moisture on the inorganic world. Then organic development continues on essentially the same path it started on. Lamarck believed that lions and so on, if destroyed, would be replaced in the course of time. There is therefore no reason to believe, for example, that today's mammals and today's fish have common ancestors—they are merely at different stages on the scale of being.

We should note Lamarck's attitude toward the fossil record in the *Philosophie zoologique*. If one believes in an evolution from simplest forms up to today's most complex forms, one might expect the record to confirm this sequence. Lamarck could perhaps not expect unambiguous progression, both because of irregularities and because he believed that through the ages new organisms were constantly appearing and starting to climb. But, assuming life did start at some first point, he might have expected some kind of progressive record. (The notion of "progression" is as crucial to our story as it is difficult to define. Although we shall see the idea evolve, for now let us understand it as a sequence from simple to complex, from the primitive to the most sophisticated, with man as the climax).

But Lamarck himself did not argue that life should have left a progressive record, nor did he bother to interpret the actual fossil record so as to support his position. Even though fossils may have triggered his evolutionism, in his theorizing, his reference to the fossil record was perfunctory at best. Noting that there are organisms in the record that apparently no longer exist, Lamarck argued briefly that since their potential rate of increase is far too great for them to have been eliminated, they must have evolved into today's forms. All Lamarck needed for this argument is that fossil forms differ from today's organisms; there is no inherent need for a progressive difference. Incidentally, given his escalator type of evolution, he found any kind of permanent complete extinction a problem—even the extinction where one organism evolves into another—and he went so far as to doubt that it occurs.

Lamarck's View of God

Finally, Lamarck presented himself as a kind of deist—as believing in God as an unmoved mover, creator of the world and its laws, who refuses to intervene miraculously in his creation. He made unselfconscious references to this God but made no stringent attempts to relate him to his creation or to read his existence and nature from it. Therefore Lamarck felt no compelling urge to prove that every useful characteristic of an organism—every "adaptation"—is evidence of God's beneficent design. Lamarck may have been an implicit teleologist in supposing some vague principle of progress, but he did not suppose that God keeps fiddling with his creation, constantly stepping in to mold organisms and their characteristics to some new ends.

Indeed, one of the curious features of the *Philosophie zoologique* is Lamarck's nonchalant attitude toward adaptation. If an organism needs something, apparently it will get it. As we have just seen from his reference to the fossil record, there is no question that a species will be wiped out because it lacks some characteristic or because it fails to change over time. Lamarck took it as more or less certain that organisms have or will attain what it takes to get along in their environments. Consequently, though it is obvious that in one sense adaptation was crucial to Lamarck, in that his whole theory was designed to show how organisms keep adapting as their environment sets up needs that trigger change, in another sense it was not of special note. Certainly adaptation ought not to be the focal point of any biological inquiry into why only some organisms have the adaptations they require. Moreover, although Lamarck was aware that organisms compete for resources, perhaps even killing and eating each other (though he doubted this happened within a species), except possibly when man interferes he considered this no real threat to the losers as a group—it merely keeps their numbers within bounds.

Darwin's Voyage of Discovery

By Jonathan Weiner

As a young man of twenty-two, Charles Darwin set off on a five-year journey around the world as a volunteer naturalist aboard the HMS *Beagle.* Along the way, he collected specimens of birds, plants, and animals, and kept a diary of his observations. His theory of evolution has its roots in this voyage. In the following selection Jonathan Weiner describes Darwin's experiences when he reached the Galápagos Islands, located off the western coast of South America. There Darwin collected various organisms, including finches, each of which appeared well adapted to its particular environment and distinctive from finches on the mainland. Much mythology has grown up around these birds, Weiner writes. Popular belief has it that upon viewing the finches Darwin immediately began to muse on how each type evolved from a common ancestor that migrated from South America. In reality, Weiner says, Darwin did not at first recognize the importance of the birds. Only after his return to England and the analysis of his specimens by other experts did the significance of the finches begin to dawn on him. Nevertheless, Weiner observes, the Galápagos experience did stimulate new thoughts in Darwin's mind. On the voyage home, Darwin began to speculate about what it would mean if the prevailing ideas about fixed species turned out to be wrong. Jonathan Weiner, a former science magazine writer and editor, is author of several books on scientific topics, including *The Beak of the Finch: A Story of Evolution in Our Time*, from which this selection is excerpted.

As he had done all along the voyage, Darwin collected diligently in the Galápagos: "Fish in Spirits of Wine," "Reptiles in Spirits of Wine," "Insects in Spirits of Wine," and so on. He also shot a total of thirty-one finches, representing nine kinds, from three of the four islands he visited, and he stowed them all away aboard the *Beagle*. (He had learned how to stuff birds from a freed black American slave, John Edmonstone, who gave cheap taxidermy lessons at the Edinburgh Museum.)

All this matters so much to the course of human thought that the historian Frank J. Sulloway spent fourteen years figuring out what happened and what did not happen in the islands, nailing down the story finch by finch. Thanks to his detective work, the episode is now not only one of the most famous but one of the best-documented turning points in the history of science.

Muddled About Finches

Contrary to legend, Sulloway has shown, Darwin did not think the finches were very important. He did not even think they were all finches. The cactus finch looked to him like some kind of black-bird; other finches looked like wrens and warblers. Darwin assumed there were plenty more just like them on some part of the coast of South America where the *Beagle* had failed to stop. In other words, the very quality that makes the finches so interesting now made them look like nothing special to Darwin. Their diversity disguised their uniqueness.

Much to his later regret, Darwin stored the finch specimens from his first two islands in the same bag, and he did not bother to label which bird came from where. Since conditions on the islands seemed more or less identical, he assumed the specimens were identical too.

He did notice that the mockingbirds he shot on his second island were slightly different from the mockingbirds on the first. For that reason he took the trouble to label these specimens, and all of the other mockingbirds he caught, by place of origin. But when the vice-governor of the islands told Darwin that the tortoises varied from island to island as well (claiming he could tell which island a tortoise came from by its shell), Darwin more or less ignored him. "I did not for some time pay sufficient attention to this statement," he confessed later, "and I had already partially mingled together the collections from two of the islands. I never dreamed that islands, about fifty or sixty miles apart, and most of them in sight of each other, formed of precisely the same rocks, placed under a quite similar climate, rising to a nearly equal height, would have been differently tenanted. . . ."

In short, Darwin was not yet an evolutionist; he was still partly a Creationist. He was on his way home to become a country parson. That was the career for which he had trained at Christ's College, Cambridge, where he studied Scripture and collected beetles. He was more interested in beetles than Scripture, but in those days a passion for nature was considered the perfect hobby for a parson.

The Influence of Linnaeus

Darwin in the Galápagos did not have Darwin's shoulders to stand on. He had to stand on the shoulders of the giants before him. A century before, the Swedish botanist Karl van Linné had tried, as a monumental act of religious devotion, to work out the relationships of all the living forms on earth. By doing so, Linné had hoped to glimpse the plan of the Creator, the meaning of life, much as saints and scholars looked for cosmic lessons in the relationships of all the verses, chapters, and books of the Hebrew and Greek Bibles.

Linné, who wrote under the Latin name Carolus Linnaeus, divided life on earth into kingdoms, kingdoms into classes, classes into orders, orders into genera, and genera into species. It was a system so beautiful and so convenient that all Western naturalists adopted it, although as they discovered more and more species they had to add categories. (Today the major headings are kingdom, phylum, class, order, family, genus, and species.)

Linnaeus's system is often drawn as a tree of life. The trunk of the tree divides near its base to form kingdoms, and each great trunk divides again and again into ever-finer branches and twigs: into species, subspecies, races, varieties, and, at last, like leaves on the twigs, individuals. We depict the order of life, in other words, as a family tree, a genealogy, in which the branches trace back to a common trunk. Every living thing is related, whether distantly or nearly, and every animal and plant shares the same ancestors at the root.

We have grown so accustomed to this view of life (since Darwin) that a diagram of the Galápagos finches on their evolutionary tree suggests to us instantly a family history, with a single ancestral finch multiplying and changing generation by generation so that there are now, for the moment, thirteen branches.

But that is not how Linnaeus himself saw his system. To him, and to other pious naturalists of his generation, the myriad relationships and family resemblances that Linnaeus used to bring order to nature did not represent anything like a genealogy of descent. Rather they represented the plan of God, who created the species in a single week, as described in the first pages of the Hebrew Bible: "And God created great whales . . . and every winged fowl after his kind: and God saw that it was good."

Perfect Forms

Darwin could read the story in his copy of *Paradise Lost*, which he carried with him on all his inland travels. Every kind of living thing was created in that one momentous week. It is a magnificent vision, as if the great tree of life had sprouted in an instant, breaking the ground and reaching with every branch to the creating sky; or as if all finches, lions, tigers, and oak trees were born pell-mell from the cornucopian womb of the earth, as Milton paints it:

> Innumerous living creatures, perfect forms
> Limb'd and full grown. . . .

And all these perfect forms, being perfect, had changed little or not at all since Creation day. . . .

Not everyone subscribed to this orthodox view of life. Darwin's own grandfather Erasmus argued the contrary view that life changes from generation to generation, and that the marvelous living intricacies and adaptations we see around us were built up bit by bit, rather than minted all at once. Another who argued for what we now call evolution was the great French naturalist Lamarck. A more obscure heretic was one of Darwin's teachers, Robert E. Grant. . . . Grant was more or less thrown out of scientific society for his belief that living forms change down through the generations.

Arguments like these were in the air during Darwin's student days at Edinburgh and Cambridge. Nevertheless, the orthodox view was so well accepted that most naturalists in Darwin's day, including Darwin, collected type specimens essentially two by two, one male and one female. The type was supposed to be the average, the representative, the *typical*, a specimen of God's thought at the moment of Creation. Every detail of every beetle had a sacred message if we could learn to read it; even the type of the lowliest worm had begun as a thought in the mind of God. The most glorious type of all, of course, was our own, as written in the book of Genesis: "God created man in his own image, in the image of God created he him."

Seeking Types

When Darwin collected finches, mockingbirds, and tortoises in the Galápagos, it was the type he was after: the theme, not the variations. He gathered plants and animals for the *Beagle* by the same principle that Noah collected them for the ark, two by two. Darwin in the Galápagos was still half in Milton's universe.

Besides *Paradise Lost*, Darwin brought along on the voyage the first volume of Charles Lyell's *Principles of Geology*, and although his teachers in Cambridge had warned him to take the new book with a grain of salt, Darwin had devoured it. Lyell argued that although animals and plants on this planet had indeed been created by God in an instant, and never changed since, the planet itself had been changing restlessly beneath them. Earth's crust had been rising and falling, building up and eroding everywhere since its creation. At the *Beagle's* very first stop, at St. Iago, in the Cape Verde Islands of the Atlantic, Darwin had studied the layers of coral that are exposed in the side of the island, and seen such strong evidence of gradual, geological change that he concluded more or less on the spot that Lyell was right. Thereafter everything Darwin saw in his voyage around the coast of South America confirmed and reconfirmed the then-heretical view that the earth's surface is continually created and destroyed.

Geological Views

To Darwin the idea that the sculpting of the earth's surface is still going on seemed new and outrageous. He was fascinated by the thought that in this sphere, small changes can accumulate with big effect. Lyell showed him that the creation and destruction of the earth's crust is measured not in days but in ages, and that the operation continues today at the same grand, slow pace as ever.

Mountains moved, rivers moved, oceans moved, but the species of life stayed ever the same. In the second volume of the *Principles* (which Darwin received by mail at a port in South America), Lyell savages Lamarck for suggesting the contrary. "It is idle to dispute about the abstract possibility of the conversion of one species into another," Lyell writes, "when there are known causes, so much more active in their nature, which must always intervene and prevent the actual accomplishment of such conversions." Just what those barriers are, Lyell does not say, but he is convinced they exist. "There are fixed limits beyond which the descendants from common parents can never deviate from a certain type."

That is why Darwin dropped the finches from two Galápagos islands into one bag. Like Linnaeus he was well aware that different local conditions can carve a species into local varieties. He and [*Beagle* captain] FitzRoy had already seen evidence of that in the foxes of the Falkland Islands, and Darwin thought he saw the same thing in Galápagos rats. But Darwin did not imagine that a species would split into different varieties under the near identical conditions and skies of neighboring islands; even if they had, Darwin did not imagine that such varieties would mean anything all that important.

Nine months later, the *Beagle* was on a zigzag course across the Pacific and back to England. Darwin was working on a catalogue of his ornithological specimens, including his Galápagos finches and mockingbirds, which all rode home with him in a very cramped cabin under the forecastle. A new thought struck him, and he jotted himself a note. At that moment he was working (alas for legend) on the mockingbirds.

The First Sign of Heresy

"I have specimens from four of the larger Islands," he wrote. The mockingbirds from San Cristóbal and Isabela looked about the same to him, but the specimens from Floreana and Santiago seemed different, and each kind was found exclusively on its own island. "When I recollect, the fact that from the form of the body, shape of scales & general size, the Spaniards can at once pronounce, from which Island any Tortoise may have been brought. When I see these Islands in sight of each other, & possessed of but a scanty stock of animals, tenanted by these birds, but slightly differing in structure & filling the same place in Nature, I must suspect they are only varieties."

Only varieties. If so, they would fit comfortably within the orthodox view of life. But what if they were something more than varieties? What if the mockingbirds had been blown to the Galá-

pagos from the coast of South America and then diverged from
their ancestors, generation by generation? What if there were no
limits to their divergence? What if they had diverged fast into varieties, and then gone right on diverging into species, new species,
each marooned on its own island?

"—If there is the slightest foundation for these remarks," Darwin
wrote, "the zoology of Archipelagoes—will be well worth examining; for such facts undermine the stability of Species." Then, in a
scribble that foreshadowed two decades of agonized caution, Darwin inserted a word: "would undermine the stability of Species."

Analyzing Darwin's Specimens

Darwin's collections were being talked about even before he got
off the boat, because he sent home letters and crates of specimens
during the voyage. The *Beagle* docked in Falmouth in October
1836, and (with a little diplomatic prodding from Darwin, who
was not the only explorer bearing plants and animals from the far
corners of the earth) some of the world's most learned naturalists
began poring over his finds, classifying them according to the system of Linnaeus.

On January 4, [1837] Darwin donated all of his Galápagos bird
skins (and other trophies) to the Zoological Society of London.
Within a week, specialists at the society began talking about this
new treasure trove. At the very next scheduled meeting, according to the *Proceedings of the Zoological Society*, the ornithologist
John Gould announced that he was particularly excited about "a
series of *Ground Finches*, so peculiar in form that he was induced
to regard them as constituting an entirely new group containing
14 species, and appearing to be strictly confined to the Galápagos
Islands." Gould's description of Darwin's finches made the next
morning's newspapers. The London *Daily Herald* mentioned "II
species of the birds brought back by Mr. Darwin from the Galla-
pagos [*sic*] Islands, all of which were new forms, none being previously known in this country.". . .

Separate Species

Gould summarized what he had learned so far about the Galápagos specimens. Almost all of the land birds were new, Gould said;
they had never been described before, and apparently they lived

only in the Galápagos. Three of the mockingbirds were not just local varieties, in Gould's opinion. No, as Gould had already informed the members of the Zoological Society, they were separate species. This was the verdict that Darwin had conjectured "would undermine the stability of Species."

What is more, the tame little birds that Darwin had found hopping around beneath the bushes were unique too. They were not relatives of blackbirds, warblers, wrens, and finches, as Darwin had thought when he bagged them. They were all finches, a strangely diverse group of finches, and they were all unique to the islands. Darwin squeezed in Gould's names for them on the back of his notepaper, down at the very bottom.

That was the fabulous moment—not out on the islands but indoors in a cluttered office in London. Or rather that was one in a swift series of moments, of intellectual shocks, that set Darwin reeling as expert naturalists told him more and more about his finds. The giant tortoises are unique to the Galápagos as well. So are the marine iguanas, Darwin's "imps of darkness." So are the very bushes and the cactus trees. Species after species in the Galápagos bears a family resemblance to relatives on the mainland of South America but are clearly distinct from anything ever found there. Year after year these revelations fanned the ember of Darwin's secret thought. To Darwin all these species, marooned in their lonely archipelago, had diverged from their ancestral stocks and then gone right on diverging. They had broken the species barrier.

Dawning Recognition

Darwin's fossils from South America turned out to be exciting too, although while he was digging them up and crating them he had wondered if old bones were worth the work. Many of them proved to be extinct relatives of forms. The continent of South America is the home of the armadillo, the llama, and the capybara, which is a rodent the size of a hog. Among the fossils that Darwin had found were a giant armadillo, a giant llama, and a rodent the size of a rhinoceros. These fossils helped to confirm what Lyell and other geologists had already guessed from finds in Australia. There is a "law of succession" that links the living to the dead, the same law that links the fossils of one stratum of rock to the fossils in the strata below.

If the giants he had found in the earth were ancestors of the animals he had watched on top of it, then Darwin could read in them the same thrilling story he read in the Galápagos. Whether he followed his finds horizontally, tracing the spread of animals and plants across the surface of the earth, or vertically, tracing them down into the abyss of time, the same secret stared back at him.

"It was evident that such facts as these, as well as many others, could be explained on the supposition that species gradually become modified," Darwin wrote long afterward; "and the subject haunted me." That spring he made his fast jottings about evolution in a red notebook he had started on the *Beagle*. And that summer he opened his first notebook on "Transmutation of Species."

In the memoir that he worked up from his diary, the *Journal of Researches* (better known as *The Voyage of the Beagle*), he writes at some length about the birds of the Galápagos, especially the finches, "the most singular of any in the archipelago." He notes in a famous passage that "in the thirteen species of ground-finches, a nearly perfect gradation may be traced, from a beak extraordinarily thick, to one so fine, that it may be compared to that of a warbler. I very much suspect, that certain members of the series are confined to different islands. . . ."

What follows next is the first published hint of his secret theory: "Seeing this gradation and diversity of structure in one small, intimately related group of birds, one might really fancy that, from an original paucity of birds in this archipelago, one species had been taken and modified for different ends."

Then he breaks off: "But there is not space in this work, to enter on this curious subject."

Of the Galápagos as a whole, he concludes his memoir with this tantalizing and magnificent line: "Hence, both in space and time, we seem to be brought somewhat near to that great fact—that mystery of mysteries—the first appearance of new beings on this earth."

How Life Diversifies

By Charles Darwin

Charles Darwin's *On the Origin of Species* has been called one of the most influential books of the last 150 years. From its publication in 1859, it changed thinking not only in the natural sciences but also in literature, philosophy, economics, and theology.

In the excerpt from his book that follows, Darwin sums up his theory that all plants and animals descended from a common ancestor through gradual modification over time. He starts with observations about how humans alter plants and animals by selectively breeding them, and then goes on to ask why the same force should not operate in nature. Noting that all species tend to produce more offspring than can survive, he says that inevitably a competition for resources ensues. In that competition some creatures possess traits that are better adapted to their environment than others. Those traits allow them to leave behind more offspring, some of whom inherit those key characteristics. As the environment changes, the mix of traits that lead to reproductive success also changes. In this way "natural selection," as Darwin calls it, alters the variety of traits within a species, and over time gradually leads to the division of one species into two or more new ones. For evidence of common ancestry, he points to structural similarities between human hands, the wings of bats, and the flippers of dolphins. Following this line of thought back in time, he reasons that all life on Earth descended from one "primordial form." Charles Darwin was a theology student training for the ministry when an amateur interest in biology blossomed into a lifelong passion for science.

nder domestication we see much variability. This seems to be mainly due to the reproductive system being eminently susceptible to changes in the conditions of life so that this

Charles Darwin, *On the Origin of Species by Means of Natural Selection*, 1859.

system, when not rendered impotent, fails to reproduce offspring exactly like the parent-form. . . .

Man does not actually produce variability; he only unintentionally exposes organic beings to new conditions of life, and then nature acts on the organisation, and causes variability. But man can and does select the variations given to him by nature, and thus accumulate them in any desired manner. He thus adapts animals and plants for his own benefit or pleasure. He may do this methodically, or he may do it unconsciously by preserving the individuals most useful to him at the time, without any thought of altering the breed. It is certain that he can largely influence the character of a breed by selecting, in each successive generation, individual differences so slight as to be quite inappreciable by an uneducated eye. This process of selection has been the great agency in the production of the most distinct and useful domestic breeds. . . .

There is no obvious reason why the principles which have acted so efficiently under domestication should not have acted under nature. In the preservation of favoured individuals and races, during the constantly recurrent Struggle for Existence, we see the most powerful and ever-acting means of selection. The struggle for existence inevitably follows from the high geometrical ratio of increase which is common to all organic beings. . . .

The Inevitable Competition for Survival

More individuals are born than can possibly survive. A grain in the balance will determine which individual shall live and which shall die—which variety or species shall increase in number, and which shall decrease, or finally become extinct. As the individuals of the same species come in all respects into the closest competition with each other, the struggle will generally be most severe between them; it will be almost equally severe between the varieties of the same species, and next in severity between the species of the same genus. But the struggle will often be very severe between beings most remote in the scale of nature. The slightest advantage in one being, at any age or during any season, over those with which it comes into competition, or better adaptation in however slight a degree to the surrounding physical conditions, will turn the balance.

With animals having separated sexes there will in most cases be a struggle between the males for possession of the females. The most vigorous individuals, or those which have most successfully struggled with their conditions of life, will generally leave most progeny. But success will often depend on having special weapons or means of defence, or on the charms of the males; and the slightest advantage will lead to victory.

As geology plainly proclaims that each land has undergone great physical changes, we might have expected that organic beings would have varied under nature, in the same way as they generally have varied under the changed conditions of domestication. And if there be any variability under nature, it would be an unaccountable fact if natural selection had not come into play. . . .

No Limit to Selection's Power

If then we have under nature variability and a powerful agent always ready to act and select, why should we doubt that variations in any way useful to beings, under their excessively complex relations of life, would be preserved, accumulated, and inherited? Why, if man can by patience select variations most useful to himself, should nature fail in selecting variations useful, under changing conditions of life, to her living products? What limit can be put to this power, acting during long ages and rigidly scrutinising the whole constitution, structure, and habits of each creature,—favouring the good and rejecting the bad? I can see no limit to this power, in slowly and beautifully adapting each form to the most complex relations of life. The theory of natural selection, even if we looked no further than this, seems to me to be in itself probable. . . . Let us turn to the special facts and arguments in favour of the theory.

On the view that species are only strongly marked and permanent varieties, and that each species first existed as a variety, we can see why it is that no line of demarcation can be drawn between species, commonly supposed to have been produced by special acts of creation, and varieties which are acknowledged to have been produced by secondary laws. On this same view we can understand how it is that in each region where many species of a genus have been produced, and where they now flourish, these same species should present many varieties, for where the manufactory of species has been active, we might expect, as a general rule, to find it still in action; and this is the case if varieties be incipient species. Moreover, the species of the large genera, which afford the greater number of varieties or incipient species, retain to a certain degree the character of varieties; for they differ from each other by a less amount of difference than do the species of smaller genera. The closely allied species also of the larger genera apparently have restricted ranges, and they are clustered in little groups round other species—in which respects they resemble varieties. These are strange relations on the view of each species having been independently created, but are intelligible if all species first existed as varieties. . . .

New and improved varieties will inevitably supplant and exterminate the older, less improved and intermediate varieties; and thus species are rendered to a large extent defined and distinct objects. Dominant species belonging to the larger groups tend to give birth to new and dominant forms; so that each large group tends to become still larger, and at the same time more divergent in character. But as all groups cannot thus succeed in increasing in size, for the world would not hold them, the more dominant groups beat the less dominant. This tendency in the large groups to go on increasing in size and diverging in character, together with the almost inevitable contingency of much extinction, explains the arrangement of all the forms of life, in groups subordinate to groups, all within a few great classes, which we now see everywhere around us, and which has prevailed throughout all time. This grand fact of the grouping of all organic beings seems to me utterly inexplicable on the theory of creation.

Gradual Changes

As natural selection acts solely by accumulating slight, successive, favourable variations, it can produce no great or sudden modification; it can act only by very short and slow steps. Hence the canon of 'Natura non facit saltum,' ["Nature does not move by leaps"] which every fresh addition to our knowledge tends to make more strictly correct, is on this theory simply intelligible. We can plainly see why nature is prodigal in variety, though niggard in innovation. But why this should be a law of nature if each species has been independently created, no man can explain.

Many other facts are, as it seems to me, explicable on this theory. How strange it is that a bird, under the form of woodpecker, should have been created to prey on insects on the ground; that upland geese, which never or rarely swim; should have been created with webbed feet; that a thrush should have been created to dive and feed on sub-aquatic insects; and that a petrel should have been created with habits and structure fitting it for the life of an auk or grebe! and so on in endless other cases. But on the view of each species constantly trying to increase in number, with natural selection always ready to adapt the slowly varying descendants of each to any unoccupied or ill-occupied place in nature, these facts cease to be strange, or perhaps might even have been anticipated.

Imperfections Explained

As natural selection acts by competition, it adapts the inhabitants of each country only in relation to the degree of perfection of their associates; so that we need feel no surprise at the inhabitants of any one country, although on the ordinary view supposed to have been specially created and adapted for that country, being beaten and supplanted by the naturalised productions from another land. Nor ought we to marvel if all the contrivances in nature be not, as far as we can judge, absolutely perfect; and if some of them be abhorrent to our ideas of fitness. We need not marvel at the sting of the bee causing the bee's own death; at drones being produced in such vast numbers for one single act, and being then slaughtered by their sterile sisters; at the astonishing waste of pollen by our fir-trees; at the instinctive hatred of the queen bee for her own fertile daughters; at ichneumonidae [wasps] feeding within the live bodies of caterpillars; and at other such cases. . . .

How inexplicable on the theory of creation is the oc-

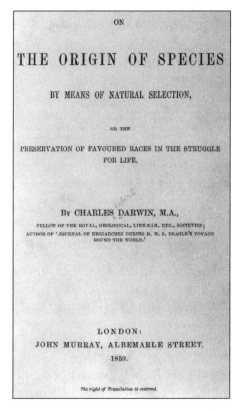

casional appearance of stripes on the shoulder and legs of the several species of the horse-genus and in their hybrids! How simply is this fact explained if we believe that these species have descended from a striped progenitor, in the same manner as the several domestic breeds of pigeon have descended from the blue and barred rock-pigeon! . . .

Instinct Subject to Selection

Glancing at instincts, marvellous as some are, they offer no greater difficulty than does corporeal structure on the theory of the natural selection of successive, slight, but profitable modifications. We can thus understand why nature moves by graduated steps in endowing different animals of the same class with their several instincts. I have attempted to show how much light the principle of gradation throws on the admirable architectural powers of the hivebee. Habit no doubt sometimes comes into play in modifying instincts; but it certainly is not indispensable, as we see, in the case of neuter insects, which leave no progeny to inherit the effects of long-continued habit. On the view of all the species of the same genus having descended from a common parent, and having inherited much in common, we can understand how it is that allied species, when placed under considerably different conditions of life, yet should follow nearly the same instincts; why the thrush of South America, for instance, lines her nest with mud like our British species. On the view of instincts having been slowly acquired through natural selection we need not marvel at some instincts being apparently not perfect and liable to mistakes, and at many instincts causing other animals to suffer. . . .

The Geological Record

If we admit that the geological record is imperfect in an extreme degree, then such facts as the record gives, support the theory of descent with modification. New species have come on the stage slowly and at successive intervals; and the amount of change, after equal intervals of time, is widely different groups. The extinction of species and of whole groups of species, which has played so conspicuous a part in the history of the organic world, almost inevitably follows on the principle of natural selection; for old forms will be supplanted by new and improved forms. Neither single species nor groups of species reappear when the chain of ordinary generation has once been broken. . . .

Looking to geographical distribution, if we admit that there has been during the long course of ages much migration from one part of the world to another, owing to former climatal and geographical changes and to the many occasional and unknown means of dispersal, then we can understand, on the theory of descent with modification, most of the great leading facts in Distribution. . . .

We see the full meaning of the wonderful fact, which must have struck every traveller, namely, that on the same continent, under the most diverse conditions, under heat and cold, on mountain and lowland, on deserts and marshes, most of the inhabitants within each great class are plainly related; for they will generally be descendants of the same progenitors and early colonists. . . .

On this view of migration, with subsequent modification, we can see why oceanic islands should be inhabited by few species, but of these, that many should be peculiar. We can clearly see why those animals which cannot cross wide spaces of ocean, as frogs and terrestrial mammals, should not inhabit oceanic islands; and why, on the other hand, new and peculiar species of bats, which can traverse the ocean, should so often be found on islands far distant from any continent. Such facts as the presence of peculiar species of bats, and the absence of all other mammals, on oceanic islands, are utterly inexplicable on the theory of independent acts of creation. . . .

The Galapagos and Mainland

It is a rule of high generality that the inhabitants of each area are related to the inhabitants of the nearest source whence immigrants might have been derived. We see this in nearly all the plants and animals of the Galapagos archipelago, of Juan Fernandez, and of the other American islands being related in the most striking manner to the plants and animals of the neighbouring American mainland; and those of the Cape de Verde archipelago and other African islands to the African mainland. It must be admitted that these facts receive no explanation on the theory of creation.

The fact, as we have seen, that all past and present organic beings constitute one grand natural system, with group subordinate to group, and with extinct groups often falling in between recent groups, is intelligible on the theory of natural selection with its contingencies of extinction and divergence of character. On these same principles we see how it is, that the mutual affinities of the species and genera within each class are so complex and circuitous. We see why certain characters are far more serviceable than others for classification;—why adaptive characters, though of paramount importance to the being, are of hardly any importance in classification; why characters derived from rudimentary parts, though of no service to the being, are often of high classificatory value; and why embryological characters are the most valuable of all. The real affinities of all organic beings are due to inheritance or community of descent. The natural system is a genealogical arrangement, in which we have to discover the lines of descent by the most permanent characters, however slight their vital importance may be.

The framework of bones being the same in the hand of a man, wing of a bat, fin of the porpoise, and leg of the horse,—the same number of vertebrae forming the neck of the giraffe and of the elephant,—and innumerable other such facts, at once explain themselves on the theory of descent with slow and slight successive modifications. The similarity of pattern in the wing and leg of a bat, though used for such different purposes,—in the jaws and legs of a crab,—in the petals, stamens, and pistils of a flower, is likewise intelligible on the view of the gradual modification of parts or organs, which were alike in the early progenitor of each class. On the principle of successive variations not always supervening at an early age, and being inherited at a corresponding not early period of life, we can clearly see why the embryos of mammals, birds, reptiles, and fishes should be so closely alike, and should be so unlike the adult forms. We may cease marvelling at the embryo of an air-breathing mammal or bird having branchial [bronchial] slits and arteries running in loops, like those in a fish which has to breathe the air dissolved in water, by the aid of well-developed branchiae. . . .

Nature may be said to have taken pains to reveal, by rudimentary organs and by homologous structures, her scheme of modification, which it seems that we wilfully will not understand.

Dealing with Doubts

I have now recapitulated the chief facts and considerations which have thoroughly convinced me that species have changed, and are still slowly changing by the preservation and accumulation of successive slight favourable variations. Why, it may be asked, have all the most eminent living naturalists and geologists rejected this view of the mutability of species? It cannot be asserted that organic beings in a state of nature are subject to no variation; it cannot be proved that the amount of variation in the course of long ages is a limited quantity; no clear distinction has been, or can be, drawn between species and well-marked varieties. It cannot be maintained that species when intercrossed are invariably sterile, and varieties invariably fertile; or that sterility is a special endowment and sign of creation. The belief that species were immutable productions was almost unavoidable as long as the history of the world was thought to be of short duration; and now that we have acquired some idea of the lapse of time, we are too apt to assume, without proof, that the geological record is so perfect that it would have afforded us plain evidence of the mutation of species, if they had undergone mutation.

But the chief cause of our natural unwillingness to admit that one species has given birth to other and distinct species, is that we are always slow in admitting any great change of which we do not see the intermediate steps. The difficulty is the same as that felt by so many geologists, when [geologist Charles] Lyell first insisted that long lines of inland cliffs had been formed, and great valleys excavated, by the slow action of the coast-waves. The mind cannot possibly grasp the full meaning of the term of a hundred million years; it cannot add up and perceive the full effects of many slight variations, accumulated during an almost infinite number of generations.

Although I am fully convinced of the truth of the views given in this volume under the form of an abstract, I by no means expect to convince experienced naturalists whose minds are stocked with a multitude of facts all viewed, during a long course of years, from a point of view directly opposite to mine. It is so easy to hide our ignorance under such expressions as the 'plan of creation,' 'unity of design,' &c., and to think that we give an explanation when we only restate a fact. Any one whose disposition leads him to attach more weight to unexplained difficulties than to the explanation of a certain number of facts will certainly reject my theory. A few naturalists, endowed with much flexibility of mind, and who have already begun to doubt on the immutability of species, may be influenced by this volume; but I look with confidence to the future, to young and rising naturalists, who will be able to view both sides of the question with impartiality. Whoever is led to believe that species are mutable will do good service by conscientiously expressing his conviction; for only thus can the load of prejudice by which this subject is overwhelmed be removed. . . .

Common Ancestor

It may be asked how far I extend the doctrine of the modification of species. The question is difficult to answer, because the more distinct the forms are which we may consider, by so much the arguments fall away in force. But some arguments of the greatest weight extend very far. . . .

Throughout whole classes various structures are formed on the same pattern, and at an embryonic age the species closely resemble each other. Therefore I cannot doubt that the theory of descent with modification embraces all the members of the same class. I believe that animals have descended from at most only four or five progenitors, and plants from an equal or lesser number.

Analogy would lead me one step further, namely, to the belief that all animals and plants have descended from some one prototype. But analogy may be a deceitful guide. Nevertheless all living things have much in common, in their chemical composition, their germinal vesicles, their cellular structure, and their laws of growth and reproduction. We see this even in so trifling a circumstance as that the same poison often similarly affects plants and animals; or that the poison secreted by the gall-fly produces monstrous growths on the wild rose or oak-tree. Therefore I should infer from analogy that probably all the organic beings which have ever lived on this earth have descended from some one primordial form, into which life was first breathed. . . .

The whole history of the world, as at present known, although of a length quite incomprehensible by us, will hereafter be recognised as a mere fragment of time, compared with the ages which have elapsed since the first creature, the progenitor of innumerable extinct and living descendants, was created.

In the distant future I see open fields for far more important researches. Psychology will be based on a new foundation, that of the necessary acquirement of each mental power and capacity by gradation. Light will be thrown on the origin of man and his history. . . .

Grandeur in the Evolutionary View

It is interesting to contemplate an entangled bank, clothed with many plants of many kinds, with birds singing on the bushes, with various insects flitting about, and with worms crawling through the damp earth, and to reflect that these elaborately constructed forms, so different from each other, and dependent on each other in so complex a manner, have all been produced by laws acting around us. These laws, taken in the largest sense, being Growth with Reproduction; inheritance which is almost implied by reproduction; Variability from the indirect and direct action of the external conditions of life, and from use and disuse; a Ratio of Increase so high as to lead to a Struggle for Life, and as a consequence to Natural Selection, entailing Divergence of Character and the Extinction of less-improved forms. Thus, from the war of nature, from famine and death, the most exalted object which we are capable of conceiving, namely, the production of the higher animals, directly follows. There is grandeur in this view of life, with its several powers, having been originally breathed into a few forms or into one; and that, whilst this planet has gone cycling on according to the fixed law of gravity, from so simple a beginning endless forms most beautiful and most wonderful have been, and are being, evolved.

Darwin's Doppelgänger

By Bert James Loewenberg

Many years passed between the end of Charles Darwin's voyage on the HMS *Beagle* in 1836 and the publication of his groundbreaking book *On the Origin of Species* in 1859. According to Bert James Loewenberg in the following selection, it might have taken longer still if not for the remarkable research of another British naturalist, Alfred Russel Wallace.

While exploring the profusion of life in South America and South Asia, Wallace wrote papers that advanced ideas very similar to Darwin's. Loewenberg writes that both Wallace and Darwin found the Galápagos Islands a particularly striking example of how varying geography gives rise to new species as plants and animals adapt to new environments. The geologist Charles Lyell, knowing that Wallace was on the same track that Darwin had started down in 1842, urged his friend Darwin to publish his book on natural selection as quickly as possible. To be fair to both men, in 1858 Lyell arranged for Darwin and Wallace to jointly submit papers on natural selection to London's leading biological society. The following year Darwin published the book that gained him lasting credit for evolutionary theory. Bert James Loewenberg, a historian at Sarah Lawrence College, was chairman of the Darwin Anniversary Committee. His 1959 book *Darwin, Wallace, and the Theory of Natural Selection*, from which this selection is excerpted, was published on the centennial anniversary of the publication of *Origin of Species*.

"I am working very steadily at my big book," wrote Charles Darwin to Sir Charles Lyell on November 10, 1856. "I have found it quite impossible to publish any preliminary essay or sketch; but am doing my work as completely as my pre-

Bert James Loewenberg, *Darwin, Wallace, and the Theory of Natural Selection*. Cambridge, MA: Arlington Books, 1959.

sent materials allow and without waiting to perfect them. And this much acceleration I owe to you." Darwin was always working steadily at the "big book." He was perpetually finding it impossible to publish although he wrote a preliminary sketch in 1842 and a preliminary essay in 1844. There was forever another experiment to perform, another quarry of fact to mine, a new line of analysis to pursue. When in 1856 he was finally ready to write without waiting to perfect his materials, it was in large measure due to Lyell.

Lyell's pressure was hard to resist and Darwin, having advanced all plausible objections, capitulated. But he continued to nurse every reservation, for he simply did not feel ready to announce his theory until each point was buttressed to the hilt of argument. Sir Charles Lyell, a leading British geologist, and Dr. Joseph Hooker, a leading British botanist, were already privy to Darwin's heresy on the species question. While both were receptive, they required more than mere plausibility before renouncing the regnant faith in immutability. They were impatient, moreover, to see so enticing a speculation solidly demonstrated.

A Rival in the Wings

More than intellectual curiosity accounts for the solicitude of Darwin's friends. Lyell in particular feared that someone might anticipate him. The very year before Lyell commenced to badger Darwin, he had read a significant article provocatively entitled "On the Law which has regulated the Introduction of New Species," a paper which appeared in the *Annals and Magazine of Natural History* and was filled with pertinent data and unusual observations. "*Every species*," declared the author, Alfred Russel Wallace then collecting species in far-off Borneo, "*has come into existence coincident both in space and time with a pre-existing closely-allied species.*" Lyell sent the piece to Darwin. Although Wallace's article was itself a warning, Lyell added one of his own.

Wallace's paper on the introduction of new species published in 1855 impressed Darwin but aroused no feeling of intellectual competition. On the contrary he welcomed it with his customary warmth and generosity. "I agree to the truth of almost every word," he wrote, approbation which Wallace, cut off from books, museums, and scholars, found more than palatable. "It is rare," Darwin continued, "to find oneself agreeing pretty closely with any theoretical paper; for it is lamentable how each man draws his own different conclusions from the very same facts." Wallace could hardly imagine himself the rival of a naturalist who reported that he had been working twenty years "on the question how and in what way . . . species and varieties differ from each other." Some months later, December 22, 1857, Darwin wrote another letter to Wallace. Again the older scholar commended the younger student. "I am glad that you are attending to distribution in accordance with theoretical ideas. I am a firm believer that without speculation there is no good and original observation." He welcomed Wallace into the select fraternity of naturalists whose interests took them "beyond the mere description of species." Wallace's work in no way disturbed Darwin's unhurried calm. "My work . . . will not fix or settle anything; but I hope it will aid by giving a large collection of facts, with one definite end." The book, he told Wallace, was progressing. "I have got about half written; but I do not suppose I shall publish under a couple of years." He expressed the hope that Wallace would get on with the publication of his travels from which Darwin expected to garner "a large harvest of facts."

Complementary Pursuits

Wallace was no more ruffled than Darwin. That both were immersed in similar problems was more of an advantage than a disadvantage. Both thought of cooperation, not conflict. Both were thinking in terms of the advancement of science, not in terms of the priority of publication. "I have been gratified by a letter from Darwin," Wallace wrote jubilantly, for he looked to the completion of Darwin's work with an eagerness unalloyed by rivalry. Darwin's book would save Wallace labor just as Wallace's book would supply Darwin's insatiable need for facts. Wallace saw in Darwin's activity the possibility that might "save me the trouble of writing more on my hypothesis, by proving that there is no difference in nature between the origin of species and of varieties. . . ." Should Darwin's final conclusion lead in another direction, Darwin's data would still be of inestimable value. In either case, Wallace could not fail to benefit.

Nor did Darwin fail to benefit from Wallace. Lyell's promptings were not without effect, but it was Wallace who was responsible for Darwin's mercurial acceleration. Darwin received Wallace's major paper on natural selection in June, 1858; in November, 1859 the

Origin of Species was published. Lyell's gentle prodding induced Darwin to quicken his pace. Knowledge of Wallace's independent discovery of the concept of natural selection forced Darwin to announce his theory of evolution to the scientific world and to bring his long-projected volume to completion. From Darwin's point of view the *Origin of Species* was premature. He did not feel prepared to publish and only the force of Wallace's unheralded pressure coerced him into reluctant consent.

Chasing Perfection

Lyell succeeded in making Darwin think in terms of publication, but he did not succeed in altering the image of the book Darwin intended to write. "I am working very hard at my book," he told W. D. Fox in a letter dated February 8, 1858, "but I shall not go to press at the soonest for a couple of years. . . ." Darwin described the volume of his perfectionist dreams. "It will be very big," for he became more and more entranced with his data and "the way facts fall into groups." He felt, like Croesus, overwhelmed by his "riches in facts" and he vowed that he would use them to the full. "I mean to make my book as perfect as ever I can." The *Origin of Species* of 1859 was not Darwin's conception of the perfect book nor was it as conclusive as he thought he could make it. For him it remained an "abstract" just as all his subsequent works were further amplifications of the grand idea.

Darwin's letters accurately reveal the measure of his intent. He had been gathering material on the transmutation of plant and animal forms from the time he opened his first "notebook" on species in 1837. There is good logic for beginning the period of data gathering with the epoch-making *Beagle* voyage during the years from 1831 to 1836. At what precise date Darwin abandoned the concept of fixity of species for the concept of the mutability of species is of less moment than the fact that the *Beagle* experience was vital in the transition.

Preoccupation, not procrastination, deferred the appearance of the species book. To think of the species work as delayed in any literal sense is to distort the meaning of Darwin's intellectual life. What became the *Origin of Species* was germinating in Darwin's mind from the day of the *Beagle* to the day of the crucial Wallace letter in 1858. Project followed project in a tight sequence of purpose. Experiment followed experiment, books and papers succeeded hypothetical explorations and mounting data. . . .

The *Origin of Species* would certainly have appeared without the dramatic intervention of Alfred Russel Wallace. But it is equally certain that it would have been a much larger and therefore a somewhat different book.

The Lesser-Known Naturalist

Alfred Russel Wallace still remains a relatively unknown figure. He is hardly more than a character in the legend of which Charles Darwin is the hero. No theory attaches to his name and few aspects of his experience unrelated to Darwin and Darwinism have merged into the substance of his memory. He created his own historical image by his conduct. As the independent discoverer of the theory of natural selection who unreservedly acknowledged Darwin's priority and forever after acclaimed him, he emerged as the model of the model scientist, a gracious, self-effacing scholar content to follow truth irrespective of personal aspirations. Even those spectacular phases of his career—his dissent from Darwin on the origin of man, his espousal of spiritualism, his part in the crusade against vaccination, and his advocacy of socialism—are only occasionally recalled. Yet Wallace outlived Darwin for thirty-one years, years devoted to substantial research in evolution and to a substantial fulfillment of his goals. Much of his life was quietly spectacular which explains his habits of character and his traits of mind. It was these traits and habits which made him like Darwin a great man and a great naturalist.

Wallace was born January 8, 1823 in a small Monmouthshire village of Usk. Unlike Darwin whose course was never troubled by financial cares, Wallace was almost never free of them. The *Beagle* voyage behind him, Darwin was already preparing his *Journal* for publication in 1837, when Wallace, then fourteen, commenced to support himself. Wallace's formal schooling was over, but his education had just begun. From his brother Wallace learned the surveyor's art, together with a knowledge of the elements of science basic to it. Surveying gave him a practical knowledge and sharpened his powers of perception. Contact with the countryside of southern England and Wales stimulated an appreciation for nature and incited an amateur interest in geology and the collection of species.

Chance periodically intruded upon the life of Wallace and almost deprived him of what was to become his true career. Were Darwin's father to have had his domineering way, Charles would have followed him and his illustrious grandfather, Dr. Erasmus Darwin, in the practice of medicine. The magical personality of John Stevens Henslow, man of God and man of science, transformed Charles Darwin. Until Henslow tapped his imagination and made him aware of the possibilities of science, Darwin was an aimless Cambridge undergraduate. He had decided to take holy orders as the only compromise he was able to make with parental wishes and with his own sense of duty. Henslow brought Darwin the opportunity of the *Beagle*, and the *Beagle* experience made Darwin a scientist.

Wallace was likewise caught in a tangle of fortuities. Need rather than indecision, however, caused him to meander from calling to craft and from craft to calling. But like Darwin he had first to find an opportunity before he could find himself. Before entering upon his surveying apprenticeship, he had spent a twelvemonth with an older brother in the building trade. When his surveyor brother could no longer afford to keep him, he kept himself by working with a watchmaker. He might well have continued in this profession had not his employer abandoned the business. Thereafter he spent a year at teaching only to return to surveying for another brief span. Finally, as in the case of Darwin, Wallace was stimulated by a man enraptured by nature and was himself induced to make the life of science his own.

Wallace's Mentor

If Charles Darwin had his Henslow, Alfred Russel Wallace had his Bates. Two years Wallace's junior, Henry Walter Bates was born in Leicester, February 8, 1825. The son of a manufacturer, Bates was marked for collaboration with his father in the making of hosiery, but his passion for species made him collaborate with Wallace instead. Although Wallace and Bates were both collectors, Bates was the superior in his knowledge of the collector's technique and in his understanding of general biology. When in 1844, the two first met, Bates initiated Wallace into his private world of beetles and butterflies. The friendship culminated four years later in a voyage of exploration. Carefully planned, the Amazon region was chosen because it was largely unexplored and because it offered prospects of discovering hitherto unknown fauna and flora. Bates remained in South America for more than a decade, and upon his return to England in 1864 he was appointed Secretary of the Royal Geographical Society, a post he retained until his death in 1894. Before he returned from the New World and partly as a result of Darwin's repeated urging, he published *Naturalist on the River Amazons*, one of the most notable English volumes of its kind.

Adventures at Sea

Exploration in South America was the making of Bates as it was the making of Darwin and Wallace. After arriving in London on October 5, 1852, Wallace had ample reason to confine scholarly exploration to the *terra firma* of England. Darwin's suffering from sea sickness aboard the *Beagle* made him a confirmed landlubber, but Wallace, having suffered the trauma of shipwreck, tempted the ocean again. Wallace and his companions spent seventy perilous days at sea on their homeward journey as compared with twenty-nine days on the passage out from England. About three weeks after the departure from America, fire broke out aboard the *Helen* and Wallace and the other members of the ship's company survived ten unforgettable days and nights in open boats before they were picked up some two hundred miles off the coast of Bermuda. The remainder of the trip was accomplished in an ancient vessel no longer seaworthy which, after buffeting storms and hurricanes, finally crawled into port.

Wallace accepted these adventures with a calm and fortitude that endeared him to his friends. He endured the hardships and sorrowed over the loss of his personal possessions particularly "some new-shoes, cloth coat and trousers, hat, etc." which he realized in retrospect he might have saved. The loss of his treasured collections, notes, and sketches were truly irreplacable. "My collections . . . were in the hold, and were irretrievably lost. And now I began to think that almost all the reward of my four years of privation and danger was lost. What I had hitherto sent home had little more than paid my expenses, and what I had with me in the *Helen* I estimated would have realized about £500." This was a reeling blow for one whose pounds were literally made up of hard-earned pence, but the blows of this experience continued to rain on Wallace's unbowed head. "All this," he recorded truthfully in the very year of its occurence, "might have gone with little regret."

It was the destruction of his beloved specimens which made him wince. The "insects and birds" in his possession when he left South America comprising "hundreds of new and beautiful species" had been carefully stowed away on the boat. These, he "had fondly hoped," would have made a "cabinet, as far as regards American species, one of the finest in Europe." In addition, his drawings, his notes, his jottings on natural history, and "the three most interesting years" of his journal either went up in the smoke of the fire or down to the bottom of the sea in what remained of the *Helen.* "I have need of philosophic resignation to bear my fate with patience and equanimity."

Patience and equanimity were prime Wallace virtues. The elixir of rest, the pleasures of food plus visits to tailor and haberdasher quickly refreshed him. After he was reunited with relatives and what had been salvaged of his collections he was completely restored. He set to work on classifying his materials, wrote an account of his travels, and studied species at the Linnean Society, the British Museum, and in the gardens at Kew. For eighteen months after his return to England in October, 1852, except for a trip to Switzerland in the fall of 1853, he made the birds and insects of the museums his companions and the members of the Zoological and Entomological Societies his friends. At one of the meetings of the Zoological Society, in December, 1852, he met Thomas Henry Huxley whose lucidity as a lecturer and brilliance as a young naturalist lastingly impressed him. Wallace, however, acquired other impressions and had already reached a final conclusion.

Devoted to Nature

He had concluded that the study of natural history was his very life. And he also concluded that an enticing place to continue his search for rare specimens was the Malayan Archipelago. Except for the island of Java, little of the territory had been systematically explored for scientific purposes. As an established collector with two books to his credit, it was comparatively simple to effectuate his plans. Through the good offices of Sir Roderick Murchison, President of the Royal Geographical Society, he secured passage on the gunboat *Frolic* bound for Singapore in January, 1854. The next eight years were spent in Malaya where Wallace continued his scientific education begun in South America. He covered fourteen thousand miles in the Archipelago itself, made between sixty and seventy separate execursions, and collected one hundred and twenty-five thousand six hundred and sixty specimens. Here he gathered the data which furnished the basis for much of his later work. It was here that the idea of transmutation cascaded out of his churning thoughts and disordered the metered pace of Darwin's existence.

The more Wallace collected and classified the more he was struck by the geographical distribution of species and by the differences existing among them. Even before the South American venture, he became interested in speculative questions relating to species. As early as 1847 he debated the theoretical propositions of Robert Chambers' *Vestiges of the Natural History of Creation* in his correspondence with Bates. He was more favorably disposed to the evolutionary notions presented in the *Vestiges* than were most of his contemporaries. Long afterward he commented on these ideas. "I was already speculating upon the origin of species, and taking note of everything bearing upon it that came in my way." Wallace's recollection is accurate. In another letter to Bates written that year he complained that little was to be achieved by "a mere local collection." For such restricted study he would substitute a full-dress analysis of a whole species family "principally with a view to the theory of the origin of species." By this time he was not only committed to science, but to a scientific problem which he defined as his "favourite subject—the variations, arrangements, distribution, etc., of species." Wallace's essay, "The Law which has regulated the Introduction of New Species," published the year after his arrival in Malaya, was the normal development of this interest.

Thinking like Darwin

Wallace's thinking in the 1865 essay strikingly parallels Darwin's earlier speculative progress. Both found the conventional conceptual devices of classification singularly unhelpful. These devices were in fact confusing since understanding actually decreased as knowledge of distribution of plants and animals increased. "None of the explanations attempted from the time of Linnaeus . . . have given a cause sufficient to account for the facts known at the time, or comprehensive enough to include all the new facts which have since been, and are daily being added." Charles Lyell's evolutionary geology provided both Wallace and Darwin with a controlling idea. "Geological investigations . . . have shown that the present state of the earth, and the organisms now inhabiting it, are but the last stage of a long and uninterrupted series of changes which it has undergone. . . ." This being the geological case it followed that to treat the data of geographical distribution "without any reference to these changes (as has frequently been done) must lead to very imperfect and erroneous conclusions. . . . Wallace cited his conclusions in ten succinct and summary propositions under the categories of Geography and Geology. . . ."

Wallace's Law

Wallace's law ["that every species has come into existence coincident both in time and space with a pre-existing closely allied species"] had obvious hypothetical advantages. The law helped him to understand things otherwise incomprehensible. It explained what he called "the system of natural affinities." With the aid of the law he could see a fertile connection between orders of species "each one having had for its immediate antitype a clearly allied species existing at the time of its origin. . . ." Wallace was examining his materials from many angles, and then examining them again. He was struggling to formulate a broadly encompassing idea, but it was to take another two years before he could articulate his hypothesis with clarity. "There constantly occur two or more modifications of an organ or modifications of two distinct organs, leading us on to two distinct series or species, which at length differ so much from each other as to form distinct genera or families." Wallace was clearly on the verge of a theory of natural selection. Geographical distribution was "beautifully in accordance with" his principle of synthesis. "A country," he reported with the weight of his expert authority, "having species, genera, and whole families peculiar to it, will be the necessary result of its having been isolated for a long period sufficient for many series of species to have been created on the type of pre-existing ones. . . ." The latter, having in the course of time, become extinct, give their descendents an illusory appearance of uniqueness. The instance of the Galapagos Islands excited him as they had earlier excited Darwin. These he described as "a volcanic group of high antiquity . . . probably never . . . more closely connected with the continent than they are at present" and originally populated "by the action of winds and currents." Modification produced new types of species, but each had been "created . . . on the plan of pre-existing ones."

Applying the Law

Additional connections between the "law" and the facts of life crowded each other in Wallace's mind. The existence of rudi-mentary organs in plants and animals was a "necessary" deduc-tion. Without some such hypothesis they were mystifying aberra-tions, garish facts which mocked at understanding. Rhetorical questions streamed from his pen. "What are these for? What have they to do with the great laws of creation? Do they not teach us something of the system of nature? If each species has been cre-ated independently, and without any necessary relation with pre-existing species, what do these rudiments, these apparent imper-fections mean? There must be a cause for them; they must be the necessary result of some great natural law." He marshalled a sam-pling of the facts with telling effect, facts long known to all stu-dents of anatomy, physiology, and general biology. "The minute limbs hidden beneath the skin in many of the snake-like lizards, the anal hooks of the boa constrictor, the complete series of jointed finger-bones in the paddle of the Manatus [manatee] and whale, are a few of the most familiar instances. . . . Abortive stamens, rudimentary floral envelopes and undeveloped carpels, are of the most frequent occurrence."

Darwin and Wallace were exploring along parallel lines which had not yet met. Half a world separated them in space, but their general ideas were almost identical both in time and content. From Sarawak in 1855 Wallace declared it was difficult "to determine in every case whether a given relation is an analogy or an affinity. . . ." Already he was convinced that as "we go back . . . toward the common antitype, the analogy which existed between the two groups became an affinity. . . ." Darwin wrote from Kent, July 20, 1856 to [botanist] Asa Gray of Cambridge, Massachusetts: "Either species have been independently created, or they have descended from other species, like varieties from one species. . . . For to my mind to say that species were created so and so is no scientific ex-planation; only a reverent way of saying it is so and so."

Wallace like Darwin was mindful of the imperfections of the fos-sil record. "If we consider that we have only the fragments of this vast system, the stems and branches being represented by extinct species of which we have no knowledge, while a vast mass of limbs and boughs and minute twigs and scattered leaves is what we have to place in order, and determine the true position each originally occupied with regard to the others, the whole difficulty of the true Natural System of classification becomes apparent. . . ." Nor did Darwin permit either his colleagues or his readers to luxuriate in a certainty he did not share. He was equally explicit concerning imperfections, gaps, and difficulties. "I do not," he reminded Asa Gray, "much underrate the many *huge* difficulties on this view [the theory of descent through modification], but yet it seems to me to explain . . . much, otherwise inexplicable. . . ."

Darwin Moves Ahead

Wallace was ready to reject many of the implications of fixity. Specifically, he rejected "all those systems of classification which arrange species or groups in circles, as well as those which fix a definite number for the division of each group. . . ." He summarized the data which nourished his scepticism. "We have . . . never been able to find a case in which the circle has been closed by a direct affinity. In most cases a palpable analogy has been substituted, in others the affinity is very obscure or altogether doubtful. . . ." Darwin expressed the same conviction in other words. "I have," he told Asa Gray, "come to the heterodox conclusion, that there are no such things as independently created species—that species are only strongly defined varieties." Darwin, however, was able to say in 1856 what Wallace was unable to say until 1858: "I believe I see my way pretty clearly on the means used by nature to change her species and *adapt* them to the wondrous and exquisitely beautiful contingencies to which every living being is exposed. . . ."

The Threat of Darwinism

By William Jennings Bryan

The publication of Darwin's theory of evolution touched off fierce debates in theological circles. Although many religious people accepted Darwin's ideas, others saw his claim that all life developed from a common ancestor in the remote past as a direct affront to the Bible and religion generally. William Jennings Bryan, a lawyer and former presidential candidate known as "The Great Commoner," took up the cause of defending religion, as he saw it, from evolution. In the selection that follows, Bryan writes that the teaching of evolution destroys Christian faith. He argues that evolution should be banned from public schools as atheistic doctrine unwelcome to the taxpayers who pay for education. Allowing Darwinism to flourish, he says, will lead to a breakdown of morality and a loss of hope. William Jennings Bryan, born in 1860, achieved fame as a populist politician and firebrand orator with his 1896 "Cross of Gold" speech at the Democratic national convention. He later took up a crusade against the teaching of evolution, and in 1925 became one of the prosecutors in the infamous "Monkey Trial," in which John Scopes was convicted of teaching evolution in contravention of Tennessee law. The conviction was overturned by the state's supreme court.

A boy is born in a Christian family; as soon as he is able to join words together into sentences his mother teaches him to lisp the child's prayer: "Now I lay me down to sleep; I pray the Lord my soul to keep; if I should die before I wake, I pray the Lord my soul to take."....

He talks with God. He goes to Sunday school and learns that the Heavenly Father is even more kind than earthly parents; he hears the preacher tell how precious our lives are in the sight of God—how even a sparrow cannot fall to the ground without His

William Jennings Bryan, *The Menace of Darwinism*. New York: Revell Co., 1921.

notice. All his faith is built upon the Book that informs him that he is made in the image of God; that Christ came to reveal God to man and to be man's Saviour.

Then he goes to college and a learned professor leads him through a book 600 pages thick, largely devoted to resemblances between man and the beasts about him. His attention is called to a point in the ear that is like a point in the ear of the ourang [orang-utan], to canine teeth, to muscles like those by which a horse moves his ears.

He is then told that everything found in a human brain is found in miniature in a brute brain.

Our Moral Compass Is Lost

And how about morals? He is assured that the development of the moral sense can be explained on a brute basis without any act of, or aid from, God. . . .

No mention of religion, the only basis for morality; not a suggestion of a sense of responsibility to God—nothing but cold, clammy materialism! Darwinism transforms the Bible into a story book and reduces Christ to man's level. It gives him an ape for an ancestor on His mother's side at least and, as many evolutionists believe, on His Father's side also.

The instructor gives the student a new family tree millions of years long, with its roots in the water (marine animals) and then sets him adrift, with infinite capacity for good or evil but with no light to guide him, no compass to direct him and no chart of the sea of life!

No wonder so large a percentage of the boys and girls who go from Sunday schools and churches to colleges (sometimes as high as seventy-five per cent.) never return to religious work. How can one feel God's presence in his daily life if Darwin's reasoning is sound? . . .

This is what the doctrine of evolution is doing for those who teach our children. They first discard the Mosaic account of man's creation, and they do it on the ground that there are no miracles. This in itself constitutes a practical repudiation of the Bible; the miracles of the Old and New Testament cannot be cut out without a mutilation that is equivalent to rejection. They reject the supernatural along with the miracle, and with the supernatural the inspiration of the Bible and the authority that rests upon inspiration.

If these believers in evolution are consistent and have the courage to carry their doctrine to its logical conclusion, they reject the virgin birth of Christ and the resurrection. They may still regard Christ as an unusual man, but they will not make much headway in converting people to Christianity, if they declare Jesus to be nothing more than a man and either a deliberate impostor or a deluded enthusiast. . . .

Restoring Sanctity

What is to be done? Are the members of the various Christian churches willing to have the power of the pulpit paralyzed by a false, absurd and ridiculous doctrine which is without support in the written Word of God and without support also in nature? Is "thus saith the Lord" to be supplanted by guesses and speculations and assumptions? I submit three propositions for the consideration of the Christians of the nation:

First, the preachers who are to break the bread of life to the lay members should believe that man has in him the breath of the Almighty, as the Bible declares, and not the blood of the brute, as

Clarence Darrow (center), was the defense attorney in the 1925 "Monkey Trial" that convicted John Scopes of teaching evolution, which at that time, violated Tennessee law.

the evolutionists affirm. He should also believe in the virgin birth of the Saviour.

Second, none but Christians in good standing and with a spiritual conception of life should be allowed to teach in Christian schools. Church schools are worse than useless if they bring students under the influence of those who do not believe in the religion upon which the Church and church schools are built. Atheism and Agnosticism are more dangerous when hidden under the cloak of religion than when they are exposed to view.

Third, in schools supported by taxation we should have a real neutrality wherever neutrality in religion is desired. If the Bible cannot be defended in these schools it should not be attacked, either directly or under the guise of philosophy or science. The neutrality which we now have is often but a sham; it carefully excludes the Christian religion but permits the use of the school-rooms for the destruction of faith and for the teaching of materialistic doctrines.

It is not sufficient to say that *some* believers in Darwinism retain their belief in Christianity; some survive smallpox. As we avoid smallpox because *many* die of it, so we should avoid Darwinism because it *leads many astray.*

If it is contended that an instructor has a right to teach anything he likes, I reply that the parents who pay the salary have a right to decide what shall be taught. To continue the illustration used above, a person can expose himself to the smallpox if he desires to do so, but he has no right to communicate it to others. So a man can believe anything he pleases but he has no right to teach it against the protest of his employers.

Acceptance of Darwin's doctrine tends to destroy one's belief in immortality as taught by the Bible. If there has been no break in the line between man and the beasts—no time when by the act of the Heavenly Father man became "a living Soul," at what period in man's development was he endowed with the hope of a future life? And, if the brute theory leads to the abandonment of belief in a future life with its rewards and punishments, what stimulus to righteous living is offered in its place? . . .

A Comparison with the Bible

As many believers in Darwinism are led to reject the Bible let me, by way of recapitulation, contrast that doctrine with the Bible:

Darwinism deals with nothing but life; the Bible deals with the entire universe—with its masses of inanimate matter and with its myriads of living things, all obedient to the will of the great Law Giver.

Darwin concerns himself with only that part of man's existence which is spent on earth while the Bible's teachings cover all of life, both here and hereafter.

Darwin begins by assuming life upon the earth; the Bible reveals the source of life and chronicles its creation.

Darwin devotes nearly all his time to man's body and to the points at which the human frame approaches in structure—though vastly different from—the brute; the Bible emphasizes man's god-like qualities and the virtues which reflect the goodness of the Heavenly Father.

Darwinism ends in self-destruction. As heretofore shown, its progress is suspended, and even defeated, by the very genius which it is supposed to develop; the Bible invites us to enter fields of inexhaustible opportunity wherein each achievement can be made a steppingstone to greater achievements still.

Darwin's doctrine is so brutal that it shocks the moral sense—the heart recoils from it and refuses to apply the "hard reason" upon which it rests; the Bible points us to the path that grows brighter with the years. . . .

The Need for a Belief in God

Darwinism puts God far away; the Bible brings God near and establishes the prayer-line of communication between the Heavenly Father and His children.

Darwinism enthrones selfishness; the Bible crowns love as the greatest force in the world.

Darwinism offers no reason for existence and presents no philosophy of life; the Bible explains why man is here and gives us a code of morals that fits into every human need.

The great need of the world to-day is to get back to God—back to a real belief in a living God—to a belief in God as Creator, Preserver and loving Heavenly Father. When one believes in a personal God and considers himself a part of God's plan he will be anxious to know God's will and to do it, seeking direction through prayer and made obedient through faith.

CHAPTER 2

The Modern Theory

An Introduction to Modern Evolutionary Biology

By Chris Colby

Chris Colby explains in the following selection that modern conceptions of evolution differ markedly from ideas in Charles Darwin's time. Without a knowledge of genes and the way genetic mutations produce species variants, Darwin was unable to understand the actual mechanisms of evolution. According to Colby, a knowledge of genetics has helped modern biologists understand that evolution occurs when there is a change in the gene pool. He explains by using an example of a certain species of moth living in England that had both light and dark types. As factories began emitting large amounts of soot during the industrial revolution, the dark moths blended better with their surroundings while the light moths, so visible against dark backgrounds, began to be eaten more often by birds. Over time more dark than light moths survived to reproduce, and the moth gene pool became dominated by dark moths. Colby's illustration shows how certain species types adapt more successfully to changes in environmental stresses and survive to pass on their genes. This process is called natural selection, one of the many mechanisms of evolution. Chris Colby was a graduate student in biology at Boston University when he wrote this essay, which has garnered considerable praise from teaching professionals.

Evolution is the cornerstone of modern biology. It unites all the fields of biology under one theoretical umbrella. It is not a difficult concept, but very few people—the majority of biologists included—have a satisfactory grasp of it. One common mistake is believing that species can be arranged on an evolutionary ladder from bacteria through "lower" animals, to "higher" animals and, finally, up to man.

Evolution Defined

Evolution is a change in the gene pool of a population over time. A gene is a hereditary unit that can be passed on unaltered for many generations. The gene pool is the set of all genes in a species or population.

The English moth, *Biston betularia*, is a frequently cited example of observed evolution. In this moth there are two color morphs, light and dark. H.B.D. Kettlewell found that dark moths constituted less than 2% of the population prior to 1848. The frequency of the dark [moths] increased in the years following. By 1898, 95% of the moths in Manchester and other highly industrialized areas were of the dark type. Their frequency was less in rural areas. The moth population changed from mostly light colored moths to mostly dark colored moths. The moths' color was primarily determined by a single gene. So, the change in frequency of dark colored moths represented a change in the gene pool. This change was, by definition, evolution.

The increase in relative abundance of the dark type was due to natural selection. The late eighteen hundreds was the time of England's industrial revolution. Soot from factories darkened the birch trees the moths landed on. Against a sooty background, birds could see the lighter colored moths better and ate more of them. As a result, more dark moths survived until reproductive age and left offspring. The greater number of offspring left by dark moths is what caused their increase in frequency. This is an example of natural selection. . . .

In order to understand evolution, it is necessary to view populations as a collection of individuals, each harboring a different set of traits. A single organism is never typical of an entire population unless there is no variation within that population. Individual organisms do not evolve, they retain the same genes throughout their life. When a population is evolving, the ratio of different genetic types is changing—each individual organism within a population does not change. For example, in the previous example, the frequency of black moths increased; the moths did not turn from light to gray to dark in concert. The process of evolution can be summarized in three sentences: Genes mutate. Individuals are selected. Populations evolve.

Evolution can be divided into microevolution and macroevolution. The kind of evolution documented above is microevolution. Larger changes, such as when a new species is formed, are called macroevolution. Some biologists feel the mechanisms of macroevolution are different from those of microevolutionary change. Others think the distinction between the two is arbitrary—macroevolution is cumulative microevolution.

The word evolution has a variety of meanings. The fact that all organisms are linked via descent to a common ancestor is often called evolution. The theory of how the first living organisms appeared is often called evolution. This should be called abiogenesis. And frequently, people use the word evolution when they really mean natural selection—one of the many mechanisms of evolution. . . .

Genetic Variation

Evolution requires genetic variation. If there were no dark moths, the population could not have evolved from mostly light to mostly dark. In order for continuing evolution there must be mechanisms to increase or create genetic variation and mechanisms to decrease it. Mutation is a change in a gene. These changes are the source of new genetic variation. Natural selection operates on this variation.

Genetic variation has two components: allelic diversity and non-random associations of alleles. Alleles are different versions of the same gene. For example, humans can have A, B or O alleles that determine one aspect of their blood type. Most animals, including humans, are diploid—they contain two alleles for every gene at every locus, one inherited from their mother and one inherited from their father. Locus is the location of a gene on a chromosome. Humans can be AA, AB, AO, BB, BO or OO at the blood group locus. If the two alleles at a locus are the same type (for instance two A alleles) the individual would be called homozygous. An individual with two different alleles at a locus (for example, an AB individual) is called heterozygous. At any locus there can be many different alleles in a population, more alleles than any single organism can possess. For example, no single human can have an A, B and an O allele. . . .

Assortative mating causes a non-random distribution of alleles at a single locus. . . . Humans mate assortatively according to race; we are more likely to mate with someone of [our] own race than another. In populations that mate this way, fewer heterozygotes are found than would be predicted under random mating. A decrease in heterozygotes can be the result of mate choice, or simply the result of population subdivision. Most organisms have a limited dispersal capability, so their mate will be chosen from the local population. . . .

Natural Selection

Some types of organisms within a population leave more offspring than others. Over time, the frequency of the more prolific type will increase. The difference in reproductive capability is called natural selection. Natural selection is the only mechanism of adaptive evolution; it is defined as differential reproductive success of pre-existing classes of genetic variants in the gene pool.

The most common action of natural selection is to remove unfit variants as they arise via mutation. In other words, natural selection usually prevents new alleles from increasing in frequency. . . .

When heterozygotes are more fit than either of the homozygotes, however, selection causes genetic variaton to be maintained. . . . This is called balancing selection. An example of this is the maintenance of sickle-cell alleles in human populations subject to malaria. Variation at a single locus determines whether red blood cells are shaped normally or sickled. If a human has two alleles for sickle-cell, he/she develops anemia—the shape of sickle-cells precludes them carrying normal levels of oxygen. However, heterozygotes who have one copy of the sickle-cell allele, coupled with one normal allele enjoy some resistance to malaria—the shape of sickled cells make it harder for the plasmodia (malaria causing agents) to enter the cell. Thus, individuals homozygous for the normal allele suffer more malaria than heterozygotes. Individuals homozygous for the sickle-cell are anemic. Heterozygotes have the highest fitness of these three types. Heterozygotes pass on both sickle-cell and normal alleles to the next generation. Thus, neither allele can be eliminated from the gene pool. The sickle-cell allele is at its highest frequency in regions of Africa where malaria is most pervasive. . . .

Selection Targets Individuals

Individuals are selected. The example I gave earlier was an example of evolution via natural selection. Dark colored moths had a higher reproductive success because light colored moths suffered a higher predation rate. The decline of light colored alleles was caused by light colored individuals being removed from the gene pool (selected against). Individual organisms either reproduce or fail to reproduce and are hence the unit of selection. . . .

Genes are not the unit of selection (because their success depends on the organism's other genes as well); neither are groups of organisms a unit of selection. There are some exceptions to this "rule," but it is a good generalization.

Organisms do not perform any behaviors that are for the good of their species. An individual organism competes primarily with others of it own species for its reproductive success. Natural selection favors selfish behavior because any truly altruistic act increases the recipient's reproductive success while lowering the donor's. Altruists would disappear from a population as the non-altruists would reap the benefits, but not pay the costs, of altruistic acts. Many behaviors appear altruistic. Biologists, however, can demonstrate that these behaviors are only apparently altruistic. Cooperating with or helping other organisms is often the most selfish strategy for an animal. This is called reciprocal altruism. A good example of this is blood sharing in vampire bats. In these bats, those lucky enough to find a meal will often share part of it with an unsuccessful bat by regurgitating some blood into the other's mouth. Biologists have found that these bats form bonds with partners and help each other out when the other is needy. If a bat is found to be a "cheater," (he accepts blood when starving, but does not donate when his partner is) his partner will abandon him. The bats are thus not helping each other altruistically; they form pacts that are mutually beneficial.

Altruism as Inclusive Fitness

Helping closely related organisms can appear altruistic; but this is also a selfish behavior. Reproductive success (fitness) has two components: direct fitness and indirect fitness. Direct fitness is a measure of how many alleles, on average, a genotype contributes to the subsequent generation's gene pool by reproducing. Indirect fitness is a measure of how many alleles identical to its own it helps to enter the gene pool. Direct fitness plus indirect fitness is inclusive fitness. J.B.S. Haldane once remarked he would gladly drown, if by doing so he saved two siblings or eight cousins. Each of his siblings would share one half his alleles; his cousins, one eighth. They could potentially add as many of his alleles to the gene pool as he could.

Natural selection favors traits or behaviors that increase a genotype's inclusive fitness. Closely related organisms share many of the same alleles. In diploid species, siblings share on average at least 50% of their alleles. The percentage is higher if the parents are related. So, helping close relatives to reproduce gets an organism's own alleles better represented in the gene pool. The benefit of helping relatives increases dramatically in highly inbred species. In some cases, organisms will completely forgo reproducing and only help their relatives reproduce. Ants, and other eusocial insects, have sterile castes that only serve the queen and assist her reproductive efforts. The sterile workers are reproducing by proxy.

The words selfish and altruistic have connotations in everyday use that biologists do not intend. Selfish simply means behaving in such a way that one's own inclusive fitness is maximized; altruistic means behaving in such a way that another's fitness is increased at the expense of one's own. Use of the words selfish and altruistic is not meant to imply that organisms consciously understand their motives.

Limits of Selection

The opportunity for natural selection to operate does not induce genetic variation to appear—selection only distinguishes between existing variants. Variation is not possible along every imaginable axis, so all possible adaptive solutions are not open to populations. To pick a somewhat ridiculous example, a steel shelled turtle might be an improvement over regular turtles. Turtles are killed quite a bit by cars these days because when confronted with danger, they retreat into their shells—this is not a great strategy against a two ton automobile. However, there is no variation in metal content of shells, so it would not be possible to select for a steel shelled turtle.

Here is a second example of natural selection. *Geospiza fortis* [a species of finch] lives on the Galapagos islands along with fourteen other finch species. It feeds on the seeds of the plant *Tribulus cistoides*, specializing on the smaller seeds. Another species, *G. Magnirostris*, has a larger beak and specializes on the larger seeds. The health of these bird populations depends on seed production. Seed production, in turn, depends on the arrival of wet season. In 1977, there was a drought. Rainfall was well below normal and fewer seeds were produced. As the season progressed, the *G. fortis* population depleted the supply of small seeds. Eventually, only larger seeds remained. Most of the finches starved; the population plummeted from about twelve hundred birds to less than two hundred. Peter Grant, who had been studying these finches, noted that larger beaked birds fared better than smaller beaked ones. These larger birds had offspring with correspondingly large beaks. Thus, there was an increase in the proportion of large beaked birds in the population the next generation. To prove that the change in bill size in *Geospiza fortis* was an evolutionary change, Grant had to show that differences in bill size were at least partially genetically based. He did so by crossing finches of various beak sizes and showing that a finch's beak size was influenced by its parents' genes. Large beaked birds had large beaked offspring; beak size was not due to environmental differences (in parental care, for example).

Less than Perfect Results

Natural selection may not lead a population to have the optimal set of traits. In any population, there would be a certain combination of possible alleles that would produce the optimal set of traits (the global optimum); but there are other sets of alleles that would yield a population almost as adapted (local optima). Transition from a local optimum to the global optimum may be hindered or forbidden because the population would have to pass through less adaptive states to make the transition. Natural selection only works to bring populations to the nearest optimal point. This idea is Sewall Wright's adaptive landscape. This is one of the most influential models that shape how evolutionary biologists view evolution.

Natural selection does not have any foresight. It only allows organisms to adapt to their current environment. Structures or behaviors do not evolve for future utility. An organism adapts to its environment at each stage of its evolution. As the environment changes, new traits may be selected for. Large changes in populations are the result of cumulative natural selection. Changes are introduced into the population by mutation; the small minority of these changes that result in a greater reproductive output of their bearers are amplified in frequency by selection.

Complex traits must evolve through viable intermediates. For many traits, it initially seems unlikely that intermediates would be viable. What good is half a wing? Half a wing may be no good for flying, but it may be useful in other ways. Feathers are thought to have evolved as insulation (ever worn a down jacket?) and/or as a way to trap insects. Later, proto-birds may have learned to glide when leaping from tree to tree. Eventually, the feathers that originally served as insulation now became co-opted for use in flight. A trait's current utility is not always indicative of its past utility. It can evolve for one purpose, and be used later for another. A trait evolved for its current utility is an adaptation; one that evolved for another utility is an exaptation. An example of an exaptation is a penguin's wing. Penguins evolved from flying ancestors; now they are flightless and use their wings for swimming.

Common Misconceptions

Selection is not a force in the sense that gravity or the strong nuclear force is. However, for the sake of brevity, biologists sometimes refer to it that way. This often leads to some confusion when biologists speak of selection "pressures." This implies that the environment "pushes" a population to a more adapted state. This is not the case. Selection merely favors beneficial genetic changes when they occur by chance—it does not contribute to their appearance. . . . Selection is not a guided or cognizant entity; it is simply an effect.

A related pitfall in discussing selection is anthropomorphizing on behalf of living things. Often conscious motives are seemingly imputed to organisms, or even genes, when discussing evolution. This happens most frequently when discussing animal behavior. Animals are often said to perform some behavior because selection will favor it. This could more accurately be worded as "animals that, due to their genetic composition, perform this behavior tend to be favored by natural selection relative to those who, due to their genetic composition, don't." Such wording is cumbersome.

To avoid this, biologists often anthropomorphize. This is unfortunate because it often makes evolutionary arguments sound silly. Keep in mind this is only for convenience of expression.

The phrase "survival of the fittest" is often used synonymously with natural selection. The phrase is both incomplete and misleading. For one thing, survival is only one component of selection—and perhaps one of the less important ones in many populations. For example, in polygynous species, a number of males survive to reproductive age, but only a few ever mate. Males may differ little in their ability to survive, but greatly in their ability to attract mates—the difference in reproductive success stems mainly from the latter consideration. Also, the word fit is often confused with physically fit. Fitness, in an evolutionary sense, is the average reproductive output of a class of genetic variants in a gene pool. Fit does not necessarily mean biggest, fastest or strongest.

Sexual Selection

In many species, males develop prominent secondary sexual characteristics. A few oft cited examples are the peacock's tail, coloring and patterns in male birds in general, voice calls in frogs and flashes in fireflies. Many of these traits are a liability from the standpoint of survival. Any ostentatious trait or noisy, attention getting behavior will alert predators as well as potential mates. How then could natural selection favor these traits?

Natural selection can be broken down into many components, of which survival is only one. Sexual attractiveness is a very important component of selection, so much so that biologists use the term sexual selection when they talk about this subset of natural selection.

Sexual selection is natural selection operating on factors that contribute to an organism's mating success. Traits that are a liability to survival can evolve when the sexual attractiveness of a trait outweighs the liability incurred for survival. A male who lives a short time, but produces many offspring is much more successful than a long lived one that produces few. The former's genes will eventually dominate the gene pool of his species. In many species, especially polygynous species where only a few males monopolize all the females, sexual selection has caused pronounced sexual dimorphism. In these species males compete against other males for mates. The competition can be either direct or mediated by female choice. In species where females choose, males compete by displaying striking phenotypic characteristics and/or performing elaborate courtship behaviors. The females then mate with the males that most interest them, usually the ones with the most outlandish displays. . . .

Mutation as a Mechanism of Change

The cellular machinery that copies DNA sometimes makes mistakes. These mistakes alter the sequence of a gene. This is called a mutation. There are many kinds of mutations. A point mutation is a mutation in which one "letter" of the genetic code is changed to another. Lengths of DNA can also be deleted or inserted in a gene; these are also mutations. Finally, genes or parts of genes can become inverted or duplicated. Typical rates of mutation are between 10^{-10} and 10^{-12} mutations per base pair of DNA per generation. . . .

Deleterious mutants are selected against but remain at low frequency in the gene pool. In diploids, a deleterious recessive mutant may increase in frequency due to drift. Selection cannot see it when it is masked by a dominant allele. Many disease causing alleles remain at low frequency for this reason. People who are carriers do not suffer the negative effect of the allele. Unless they mate with another carrier, the allele may simply continue to be passed on. Deleterious alleles also remain in populations at a low frequency due to a balance between recurrent mutation and selection. This is called the mutation load. . . .

One example of a beneficial mutation comes from the mosquito *Culex pipiens.* In this organism, a gene that was involved with breaking down organophosphates—common insecticide ingredients—became duplicated. Progeny of the organism with this mutation quickly swept across the worldwide mosquito population. There are numerous examples of insects developing resistance to chemicals, especially DDT, which was once heavily used in this country. And, most importantly, even though "good" mutations happen much less frequently than "bad" ones, organisms with "good" mutations thrive while organisms with "bad" ones die out. . . .

The general lack of large fitness differences segregating in natural populations argues that beneficial mutants do indeed arise infrequently. However, the impact of a beneficial mutant on the level of variation at a locus can be large and lasting. It takes many generations for a locus to regain appreciable levels of heterozygosity following a selective sweep. . . .

Adaptation is brought about by cumulative natural selection, the repeated sifting of mutations by natural selection. Small changes, favored by selection, can be the stepping-stone to further changes. The summation of large numbers of these changes is macroevolution.

Evidence for Evolution

By the National Academy of Sciences

In this selection the National Academy of Sciences (NAS) summarizes the many lines of evidence that support the theory of evolution. The fossil record, the NAS says, demonstrates that life has evolved in a general sequence. The oldest fossil-bearing rocks show only bacteria, newer ones reveal increasingly complex cells, and still more recent rocks bear fossils of multicellular life, including plants and animals. Another line of evidence is homology, the similar internal structures of animals. An instance of this, the NAS points out, is the skeletal similarities of diverse mammals. More recently, advances in genetic analysis have provided molecular evidence supporting evolution. These lines of evidence, according in the NAS, confirm that human beings evolved from primate ancestors, who in turn evolved from the common ancestor of all mammals. The National Academy of Sciences is a private association of distinguished scientists. Established in 1863, the NAS advises the federal government and educates the public about science and technology.

A long path leads from the origins of primitive "life," which existed at least 3.5 billion years ago, to the profusion and diversity of life that exists today. This path is best understood as a product of evolution.

Contrary to popular opinion, neither the term nor the idea of biological evolution began with Charles Darwin and his foremost work, *On the Origin of Species by Means of Natural Selection* (1859). Many scholars from the ancient Greek philosophers on had inferred that similar species were descended from a common ancestor. The word "evolution" first appeared in the English language in 1647 in a nonbiological connection, and it became

National Academy of Sciences, *Science and Creationism: A View from the National Academy of Sciences, Second Edition*. Washington, DC: National Academy Press, 1999. Copyright © 2000 by the National Academy of Sciences, courtesy of the National Academies Press, Washington, D.C. Reproduced by permission.

widely used in English for all sorts of progressions from simpler beginnings. The term Darwin most often used to refer to biological evolution was "descent with modification," which remains a good brief definition of the process today.

Darwin proposed that evolution could be explained by the differential survival of organisms following their naturally occurring variation—a process he termed "natural selection." According to this view, the offspring of organisms differ from one another and from their parents in ways that are heritable—that is, they can pass on the differences genetically to their own offspring. Furthermore, organisms in nature typically produce more offspring than can survive and reproduce given the constraints of food, space, and other environmental resources. If a particular offspring has traits that give it an advantage in a particular environment, that organism will be more likely to survive and pass on those traits. As differences accumulate over generations, populations of organisms diverge from their ancestors.

Darwin's original hypothesis has undergone extensive modification and expansion, but the central concepts stand firm. Studies in genetics and molecular biology—fields unknown in Darwin's time—have explained the occurrence of the hereditary variations that are essential to natural selection. Genetic variations result from changes, or mutations, in the nucleotide sequence of DNA, the molecule that genes are made from. Such changes in DNA now can be detected and described with great precision.

Roles of Chance and Selection

Genetic mutations arise by chance. They may or may not equip the organism with better means for surviving in its environment. But if a gene variant improves adaptation to the environment (for example, by allowing an organism to make better use of an available nutrient, or to escape predators more effectively—such as through stronger legs or disguising coloration), the organisms carrying that gene are more likely to survive and reproduce than those without it. Over time, their descendants will tend to increase, changing the average characteristics of the population. Although the genetic variation on which natural selection works is based on random or chance elements, natural selection itself produces "adaptive" change—the very opposite of chance.

Scientists also have gained an understanding of the processes by which new species originate. A new species is one in which the individuals cannot mate and produce viable descendants with individuals of a preexisting species. The split of one species into two often starts because a group of individuals becomes geographically separated from the rest. This is particularly apparent in distant remote islands, such as the Galápagos and the Hawaiian archipelago, whose great distance from the Americas and Asia means that arriving colonizers will have little or no opportunity to mate with individuals remaining on those continents. Mountains, rivers, lakes, and other natural barriers also account for geographic separation between populations that once belonged to the same species.

Once isolated, geographically separated groups of individuals become genetically differentiated as a consequence of mutation and other processes, including natural selection. The origin of a species is often a gradual process, so that at first the reproductive isolation between separated groups of organisms is only partial, but it eventually becomes complete. Scientists pay special attention to these intermediate situations, because they help to reconstruct the details of the process and to identify particular genes or sets of genes that account for the reproductive isolation between species.

A particularly compelling example of speciation involves the 13 species of finches studied by Darwin on the Galápagos Islands, now known as Darwin's finches. The ancestors of these finches appear to have emigrated from the South American mainland to the Galápagos. Today the different species of finches on the island have distinct habitats, diets, and behaviors, but the mechanisms involved in speciation continue to operate. A research group led by Peter and Rosemary Grant of Princeton University has shown that a single year of drought on the islands can drive evolutionary changes in the finches. Drought diminishes supplies of easily cracked nuts but permits the survival of plants that produce larger, tougher nuts. Droughts thus favor birds with strong, wide beaks that can break these tougher seeds, producing populations of birds with these traits. The Grants have estimated that if droughts occur about once every 10 years on the islands, a new species of finch might arise in only about 200 years.

The following sections consider several aspects of biological evolution in greater detail, looking at paleontology, comparative anatomy, biogeography, embryology, and molecular biology for further evidence supporting evolution.

The Fossil Record

Although it was Darwin, above all others, who first marshaled convincing evidence for biological evolution, earlier scholars had recognized that organisms on Earth had changed systematically over long periods of time. For example, in 1799 an engineer named William Smith reported that, in undisrupted layers of rock, fossils occurred in a definite sequential order, with more modern-appearing ones closer to the top. Because bottom layers of rock logically were laid down earlier and thus are older than top layers, the sequence of fossils also could be given a chronology from oldest to youngest. His findings were confirmed and extended in the 1830s by the paleontologist William Lonsdale, who recognized that fossil remains of organisms from lower strata were more primitive than the ones above. Today, many thousands of ancient rock deposits have been identified that show corresponding successions of fossil organisms.

Thus, the general sequence of fossils had already been recognized before Darwin conceived of descent with modification. But the paleontologists and geologists before Darwin used the sequence of fossils in rocks not as proof of biological evolution, but as a basis for working out the original sequence of rock strata that had been structurally disturbed by earthquakes and other forces.

In Darwin's time, paleontology was still a rudimentary science. Large parts of the geological succession of stratified rocks were unknown or inadequately studied.

Darwin, therefore, worried about the rarity of intermediate forms between some major groups of organisms.

Today, many of the gaps in the paleontological record have been filled by the research of paleontologists. Hundreds of thousands of fossil organisms, found in well-dated rock sequences, represent successions of forms through time and manifest many evolutionary transitions. As mentioned earlier, microbial life of the simplest type was already in existence 3.5 billion years ago. The oldest evidence of more complex organisms (that is, eucaryotic cells, which are more complex than bacteria) has been discovered in fossils sealed in rocks approximately 2 billion years old. Multicellular organisms, which are the familiar fungi, plants, and animals, have been found only in younger geological strata. . . .

So many intermediate forms have been discovered between fish and amphibians, between amphibians and reptiles, between reptiles and mammals, and along the primate lines of descent that it often is difficult to identify categorically when the transition occurs from one to another particular species. Actually, nearly all fossils can be regarded as intermediates in some sense; they are life forms that come between the forms that preceded them and those that followed.

The fossil record thus provides consistent evidence of systematic change through time—of descent with modification. From this huge body of evidence, it can be predicted that no reversals will be found in future paleontological studies. That is, amphibians will not appear before fishes, nor mammals before reptiles, and no complex life will occur in the geological record before the oldest eucaryotic cells. This prediction has been upheld by the evidence that has accumulated until now: no reversals have been found.

Common Structures

Inferences about common descent derived from paleontology are reinforced by comparative anatomy. For example, the skeletons of humans, mice, and bats are strikingly similar, despite the different ways of life of these animals and the diversity of environments in which they flourish. The correspondence of these animals, bone by bone, can be observed in every part of the body, including the limbs; yet a person writes, a mouse runs, and a bat flies with structures built of bones that are different in detail but similar in general structure and relation to each other.

Scientists call such structures homologies and have concluded that they are best explained by common descent. Comparative anatomists investigate such homologies, not only in bone structure but also in other parts of the body, working out relationships from degrees of similarity. Their conclusions provide important inferences about the details of evolutionary history, inferences that can be tested by comparisons with the sequence of ancestral forms in the paleontological record.

The mammalian ear and jaw are instances in which paleontology and comparative anatomy combine to show common ancestry through transitional stages. The lower jaws of mammals contain only one bone, whereas those of reptiles have several. The other bones in the reptile jaw are homologous with bones now found in the mammalian ear. Paleontologists have discovered intermediate forms of mammal-like reptiles (*Therapsida*) with a double jaw joint—one composed of the bones that persist in mammalian jaws, the other consisting of bones that eventually became the hammer and anvil of the mammalian ear.

The Distribution of Species

Biogeography also has contributed evidence for descent from common ancestors. The diversity of life is stupendous. Approximately 250,000 species of living plants, 100,000 species of fungi, and one million species of animals have been described and named, each occupying its own peculiar ecological setting or niche; and the census is far from complete. Some species, such as human beings and our companion the dog, can live under a wide range of environments. Others are amazingly specialized. One species of a fungus (*Laboulbenia*) grows exclusively on the rear portion of the covering wings of a single species of beetle (*Aphaenops cronei*) found only in some caves of southern France. The larvae of the fly *Drosophila carcinophila* can develop only in specialized grooves beneath the flaps of the third pair of oral appendages of a land crab that is found only on certain Caribbean islands.

How can we make intelligible the colossal diversity of living beings and the existence of such extraordinary, seemingly whimsical creatures as the fungus, beetle, and fly described above? And why are island groups like the Galápagos so often inhabited by forms similar to those on the nearest mainland but belonging to different species? Evolutionary theory explains that biological diversity results from the descendants of local or migrant predecessors becoming adapted to their diverse environments. This explanation can be tested by examining present species and local fossils to see whether they have similar structures, which would indicate how one is derived from the other. Also, there should be evidence that species without an established local ancestry had migrated into the locality.

Wherever such tests have been carried out, these conditions have been confirmed. A good example is provided by the mammalian populations of North and South America, where strikingly different native organisms evolved in isolation until the emergence of the isthmus of Panama approximately 3 million years ago. Thereafter, the armadillo, porcupine, and opossum—mammals of South American origin—migrated north, along with many other species of plants and animals, while the mountain lion and other North

American species made their way across the isthmus to the south.

The evidence that Darwin found for the influence of geographical distribution on the evolution of organisms has become stronger with advancing knowledge. For example, approximately 2,000 species of flies belonging to the genus *Drosophila* are now found throughout the world. About one-quarter of them live only in Hawaii. More than a thousand species of snails and other land mollusks also are found only in Hawaii. The biological explanation for the multiplicity of related species in remote localities is that such great diversity is a consequence of their evolution from a few common ancestors that colonized an isolated environment. The Hawaiian Islands are far from any mainland or other islands, and on the basis of geological evidence they never have been attached to other lands. Thus, the few colonizers that reached the Hawaiian Islands found many available ecological niches, where they could, over numerous generations, undergo evolutionary change and diversification. No mammals other than one bat species lived in the Hawaiian Islands when the first human settlers arrived; similarly, many other kinds of plants and animals were absent.

The Hawaiian Islands are not less hospitable than other parts of the world for the absent species. For example, pigs and goats have multiplied in the wild in Hawaii, and other domestic animals also thrive there. The scientific explanation for the absence of many kinds of organisms, and the great multiplication of a few kinds, is that many sorts of organisms never reached the islands, because of their geographic isolation. Those that did reach the islands diversified over time because of the absence of related organisms that would compete for resources.

Similarities During Development

Embryology, the study of biological development from the time of conception, is another source of independent evidence for common descent. Barnacles, for instance, are sedentary crustaceans with little apparent similarity to such other crustaceans as lobsters, shrimps, or copepods. Yet barnacles pass through a free-swimming larval stage in which they look like other crustacean larvae. The similarity of larval stages supports the conclusion that all crustaceans have homologous parts and a common ancestry.

Similarly, a wide variety of organisms from fruit flies to worms to mice to humans have very similar sequences of genes that are active early in development. These genes influence body segmentation or orientation in all these diverse groups. The presence of such similar genes doing similar things across such a wide range of organisms is best explained by their having been present in a very early common ancestor of all of these groups.

Molecular Evidence

The unifying principle of common descent that emerges from all the foregoing lines of evidence is being reinforced by the discoveries of modern biochemistry and molecular biology.

The code used to translate nucleotide sequences into amino acid sequences is essentially the same in all organisms. Moreover, proteins in all organisms are invariably composed of the same set of 20 amino acids. This unity of composition and function is a powerful argument in favor of the common descent of the most diverse organisms.

In 1959, scientists at Cambridge University in the United Kingdom determined the three-dimensional structures of two proteins that are found in almost every multicelled animal: hemoglobin and myoglobin. Hemoglobin is the protein that carries oxygen in the blood. Myoglobin receives oxygen from hemoglobin and stores it in the tissues until needed. These were the first three-dimensional protein structures to be solved, and they yielded some key insights. Myoglobin has a single chain of 153 amino acids wrapped around a group of iron and other atoms (called "heme") to which oxygen binds. Hemoglobin, in contrast, is made of up four chains: two identical chains consisting of 141 amino acids, and two other identical chains consisting of 146 amino acids. However, each chain has a heme exactly like that of myoglobin, and each of the four chains in the hemoglobin molecule is folded exactly like myoglobin. It was immediately obvious in 1959 that the two molecules are very closely related.

During the next two decades, myoglobin and hemoglobin sequences were determined for dozens of mammals, birds, reptiles, amphibians, fish, worms, and molluscs. All of these sequences were so obviously related that they could be compared with confidence with the three-dimensional structures of two selected standards—whale myoglobin and horse hemoglobin. Even more significantly, the differences between sequences from different organisms could be used to construct a family tree of hemoglobin and myoglobin variation among organisms. This tree agreed completely with observations derived from paleontology and anatomy about the common descent of the corresponding organisms. . . .

As the ability to sequence the nucleotides making up DNA has improved, it also has become possible to use genes to reconstruct the evolutionary history of organisms. Because of mutations, the sequence of nucleotides in a gene gradually changes over time. The more closely related two organisms are, the less different their DNA will be. Because there are tens of thousands of genes in humans and other organisms, DNA contains a tremendous amount of information about the evolutionary history of each organism. . . .

The evidence for evolution from molecular biology is overwhelming and is growing quickly. In some cases, this molecular evidence makes it possible to go beyond the paleontological evidence. For example, it has long been postulated that whales descended from land mammals that had returned to the sea. From anatomical and paleontological evidence, the whales' closest living land relatives seemed to be the even-toed hoofed mammals (modern cattle, sheep, camels, goats, etc.). Recent comparisons of some milk protein genes (beta-casein and kappa-casein) have confirmed this relationship and have suggested that the closest landbound living relative of whales may be the hippopotamus. In this case, molecular biology has augmented the fossil record. . . .

Human Evolution

Studies in evolutionary biology have led to the conclusion that human beings arose from ancestral primates. This association was hotly debated among scientists in Darwin's day. But today there is no significant scientific doubt about the close evolutionary relationships among all primates, including humans.

Many of the most important advances in paleontology over the past century relate to the evolutionary history of humans. Not one but many connecting links—immediate between and along various branches of the human family tree—have been found as fossils. These linking fossils occur in geological deposits of intermediate age. They document the time and rate at which primate and human evolution occurred.

Scientists have unearthed thousands of fossil specimens representing members of the human family. A great number of these cannot be assigned to the modern human species, *Homo sapiens.*

Most of these specimens have been well dated, often by means of radiometric techniques. They reveal a well-branched tree, parts of which trace a general evolutionary sequence leading from ape-like forms to modern humans.

Paleontologists have discovered numerous species of extinct apes in rock strata that are older than four million years, but never a member of the human family at that great age. *Australopithecus*, whose earliest known fossils are about four million years old, is a genus with some features closer to apes and some closer to modern humans. In brain size, *Australopithecus* was barely more advanced than apes. A number of features, including long arms, short legs, intermediate toe structure, and features of the upper limb, indicate that the members of this species spent part of the time in trees. But they also walked upright on the ground, like humans. Bipedal tracks of *Australopithecus* have been discovered, beautifully preserved with those of other extinct animals, in hardened volcanic ash. Most of our *Australopithecus* ancestors died out close to two-and-a-half million years ago, while other *Australopithecus* species, which were on side branches of the human tree, survived alongside more advanced hominids for another million years.

Distinctive bones of the oldest species of the human genus, *Homo*, date back to rock strata about 2.4 million years old. Physical anthropologists agree that *Homo* evolved from one of the species of *Australopithecus*. By two million years ago, early members of *Homo* had an average brain size one-and-a-half times larger than that of *Australopithecus*, though still substantially smaller than that of modern humans. The shapes of the pelvic and leg bones suggest that these early *Homo* were not part-time climbers like *Australopithecus* but walked and ran on long legs, as modern humans do. Just as *Australopithecus* showed a complex of ape-like, human-like, and intermediate features, so was early *Homo* intermediate between *Australopithecus* and modern humans in some features, and close to modern humans in other respects. The earliest stone tools are of virtually the same age as the earliest fossils of *Homo*. Early *Homo*, with its larger brain than *Australopithecus*, was a maker of stone tools.

The fossil record for the interval between 2.4 million years ago and the present includes the skeletal remains of several species assigned to the genus *Homo*. The more recent species had larger brains than the older ones. This fossil record is complete enough to show that the human genus first spread from its place of origin in Africa to Europe and Asia a little less than two million years ago. Distinctive types of stone tools are associated with various populations. More recent species with larger brains generally used more sophisticated tools than more ancient species.

Genetic Links with Apes

Molecular biology also has provided strong evidence of the close relationship between humans and apes. Analysis of many proteins and genes has shown that humans are genetically similar to chimpanzees and gorillas and less similar to orangutans and other primates.

DNA has even been extracted from a well-preserved skeleton of the extinct human creature known as Neanderthal, a member of the genus *Homo* and often considered either as a subspecies of *Homo sapiens* or as a separate species. Application of the molecular clock, which makes use of known rates of genetic mutation, suggests that Neanderthal's lineage diverged from that of modern *Homo sapiens* less than half a million years ago, which is entirely compatible with evidence from the fossil record.

Based on molecular and genetic data, evolutionists favor the hypothesis that modern *Homo sapiens*, individuals very much like us, evolved from more archaic humans about 100,000 to 150,000 years ago. They also believe that this transition occurred in Africa, with modern humans then dispersing to Asia, Europe, and eventually Australasia and the Americas.

Discoveries of hominid remains during the past three decades in East and South Africa, the Middle East, and elsewhere have combined with advances in molecular biology to initiate a new discipline—molecular paleoanthropology. This field of inquiry is providing an ever-growing inventory of evidence for a genetic affinity between human beings and the African apes.

How Evolution Achieves the Improbable

By Richard Dawkins

Even among scientists there are those who doubt the theory of evolution. In the following selection zoologist Richard Dawkins refutes their arguments. He claims that the doubters misunderstand the role of chance. They focus on the impossible-seeming odds of a particular organ, especially an exceedingly complex one such as the eye, emerging by chance alone. To critics, such odds seem to require an intelligent designer. This is a mistake, Dawkins says, because evolution does not rely on chance alone, but on the combination of random variation of genes and nonrandom natural selection. Heredity is key; it allows any genetic variation that confers on individuals a survival advantage to be passed down through generations. Such small improvements can over time produce complex organs such as the human eye. Trained in zoology at Oxford University, Richard Dawkins gained international renown in 1976 with the publication of his first book, *The Selfish Gene*, which crystallized the modern synthesis of Darwin's theory with genetics. His gift for explaining evolution led to his being appointed the first holder of the Charles Simonyi Chair of Public Understanding of Science at Oxford.

Mount Improbable rears up from the plain, lofting its peaks dizzily to the rarefied sky. The towering, vertical cliffs of Mount Improbable can never, it seems, be climbed. Dwarfed like insects, thwarted mountaineers crawl and scrabble along the foot, gazing hopelessly at the sheer, unattainable heights. They shake their tiny, baffled heads and declare the brooding summit forever unscalable.

Richard Dawkins, *Climbing Mount Improbable*. London, UK: Viking, Penguin Group, 1996.

Our mountaineers are too ambitious. So intent are they on the perpendicular drama of the cliffs, they do not think to look round the other side of the mountain. There they would find not vertical cliffs and echoing canyons but gently inclined grassy meadows, graded steadily and easily towards the distant uplands. Occasionally the gradual ascent is punctuated by a small, rocky crag, but you can usually find a detour that is not too steep for a fit hillwalker in stout shoes and with time to spare. The sheer height of the peak doesn't matter, so long as you don't try to scale it in a single bound. Locate the mildly sloping path and, if you have unlimited time, the ascent is only as formidable as the next step. The story of Mount Improbable is, of course, a parable. We shall [now] explore its meaning. . . .

A Letter from a Doubter

The following is from a letter that *The Times* of London published a few years ago. The author, whose name I have withheld to spare embarrassment, is a physicist, regarded sufficiently highly by his peers to have been elected a Fellow of the Royal Society, Britain's most distinguished learned institution.

> Sir, I am one of the physical scientists . . . who doubt Darwin's theory of evolution. My doubts arise not from any religious motive or desire to add fuel to either side of any controversy but merely because I think that Darwinism is scientifically indefensible.
>
> . . . We have no option but to accept evolution—all the fossil evidence points to it. The contention is only about the cause. Darwin maintains that the cause was chance: as generation succeeded generation there would be minor variations at random, those that gave some advantage would persist and those that did not would disappear. Thus living beings would gradually improve with, for example, enhanced powers of obtaining food or of destroying their enemies. This process Darwin called natural selection.
>
> As a physicist, I cannot accept this. It seems to me to be impossible that chance variation should have produced the remarkable machine that is the human body. Take only one example—the eye. Darwin admitted that this defeated him—he could not see how it could have evolved from a simple light–sensitive organ . . . I myself can see no

alternative to the hypothesis that living matter was designed. The origin of life is not explainable in terms of standard science nor is the wonderful succession of living creatures formed throughout the thousands of millions of years of this planet's existence.

But who was the Designer?

Yours faithfully,

Mistaking Evolution for Chance

The author is at pains to let us know, twice, that he is a physicist, which gives special weight to his views. Another physical scientist, a professor of chemistry at San Jose State University, California, has burst into biology with a publication called 'The Smyrna Fig requires God for its Production'. He describes the remarkable complexity of the relationship between figs and their wasp pollinators and he comes to the following conclusion: 'A young wasp lies dormant in a caprifig all winter, but hatches at the exact time to lay her eggs in the summer crop of caprifigs which is necessary to pollinate the fruit. This all requires exact timing which means God controls it'! (The exclamation mark is mine.) 'To think that all of this exact pattern resulted from evolutionary chance is preposterous. Without God nothing like the Smyrna fig could exist . . . Evolutionists pretend that things arise by chance without a definite purpose or a completely thought out plan.'

One of Britain's most famous physical scientists, Sir Fred Hoyle (incidentally the author of *The Black Cloud*, which must be among the best science-fiction novels ever written), frequently expresses a similar view with respect to large molecules such as enzymes, whose inherent 'improbability'—that is the probability that they'd spontaneously come into existence by chance—is easier to calculate than that of eyes or figs. Enzymes work in cells rather like exceedingly numerous machine tools for molecular mass production. Their efficacy depends upon their three-dimensional shape, their shape depends upon their coiling behaviour, and their coiling behaviour depends upon the sequence of amino acids which link up in a chain to make them. This exact sequence is directly controlled by genes and it really matters. Could it come about by chance?

Hoyle says no, and he is right. There is a fixed number of amino acids available, twenty. A typical enzyme is a chain of several hundred links drawn from the twenty. An elementary calculation shows that the probability that any particular sequence of, say 100, amino acids will spontaneously form is one in $20 \times 20 \times 20 \ldots$ 100 times, or 1 in 20^{100}. This is an inconceivably large number, far greater than the number of fundamental particles in the entire universe. Sir Fred, bending over backwards (unnecessarily, as we shall see) to be fair to those whom he sees as his Darwinian opponents, generously shortens the odds to 1 in 10^{20}. A more modest number to be sure, but still a horrifyingly low probability. His co-author and fellow astrophysicist, Professor Chandra Wickramasinghe, has quoted him as saying that the spontaneous formation by 'chance' of a working enzyme is like a hurricane blowing through a junkyard and spontaneously having the luck to put together a Boeing 747. What Hoyle and Wickramasinghe miss is that Darwinism is *not* a theory of random chance. It is a theory of random mutation plus *non-random* cumulative natural selection. Why, I wonder, is it so hard for even sophisticated scientists to grasp this simple point? . . .

Heredity Is a Key Step

We have identified the ingredients that must be before evolution can occur as being mutation and natural selection. These two will follow automatically on any planet given a more fundamental ingredient, one that is difficult, but obviously not impossible, to procure. This difficult basic ingredient is heredity. In order for natural selection to occur, anywhere in the universe, there must be lineages of things that resemble their immediate ancestors more than they resemble members of the population at large. Heredity is not the same thing as reproduction. You can have reproduction without heredity. Bush fires reproduce but without heredity.

Imagine a dry, parched grassland, stretching for mile after mile in every direction. Now, in a particular place, a careless smoker drops a lighted match and in no time at all the grass has flared up into a racing fire. Our smoker runs away from it as hard as his coughing lungs will let him, but we are more concerned with the way the fire spreads. It doesn't just swell steadily outwards from the original starting point. It also sends sparks up into the air. These sparks, or burning wisps of dry grass, are carried by the wind far away from the original fire. When a spark eventually comes down, it starts a new fire somewhere else on the tinder-dry prairie. And later, the new fire sends off sparks which kindle yet more new fires somewhere else. We could say that the fires are indulging in a form of reproduction. Each new fire has one parent fire. This is the fire that spat out the spark that started it. And it has one grandparent fire, one great-grandparent fire, and so on back until the ancestral fire started by the wayward match. A new fire can have only one mother but it can have more than one daughter, because it can send out more than one spark in different directions. If you watched the whole process from above and were able to record the history of each flare-up, you could draw out a complete family tree of the fires on the prairie.

Now the point of the story is that although there is reproduction among the fires there is no true *heredity*. For there to be true heredity, each fire would have to resemble its parent more than it resembled the other fires in general. There is nothing wrong with the *idea* of a fire resembling its parent. It could happen. Fires do vary, do have individual qualities, just as people do. A fire may have its own characteristic flame colour, its own smoke colour, flame size, noise level and so on. It could resemble its parent fire in any of these characteristics. If, in general, fires *did* resemble their parents in these ways, we could say that we had true heredity. But in fact fires don't resemble their parents any more than they resemble the general run of fires dotted around the prairie. An individual flare-up gets its characteristic qualities, its flame size, smoke colour, crackle volume and so on, from its surroundings; from the kind of grass that happens to be growing where the spark lands; from the dryness of the grass; from the speed and direction of the wind. These are all qualities of the local area where the spark lands. They are not qualities of the parent fire from which the spark came.

No Special Resemblance

In order for there to be true heredity, each spark would have to carry with it some quality, some characteristic essence, of its parent fire. For example, suppose that some fires have yellow flames, others red flames, others blue. Now, if yellow-flamed fires give off sparks that start new yellow-flamed fires, whereas red-flamed fires give off sparks that start new red fires, and so on, we'd have true heredity. But that isn't what happens. If we see a blue flame we say, 'There must be some copper salts in this area.' We don't say, 'This fire must have been started by a spark from another blue-flamed fire somewhere else.'

And this, of course, is where rabbits and humans and dandelions differ from fires. Don't be misled, incidentally, by the fact that rabbits have two parents and four grandparents whereas fires have only one parent and one grandparent. That is an important difference, but it is not the one we are talking about at the moment. If it helps, think not of rabbits but of stick insects or aphids, where females can have daughters, granddaughters and great-granddaughters without males ever being involved. The shape, colour, size and temperament of a stick insect is influenced, no doubt, by the place and climate of its upbringing. But it is influenced, too, by the spark that flies only from parent to child.

Flow of DNA

So what is it, this mysterious spark that flies from parent to offspring but not from fire to fire? On this planet it is DNA. The most amazing molecule in the world. It is easy to think of DNA as the information by which a body makes another body like itself. It would be more correct to see a body as the vehicle used by DNA to make more DNA like itself. All the DNA in the world at a given time, such as now, has come down through an unbroken chain of successful ancestors. No two individuals (except identical twins) have exactly the same DNA. Differences between DNA in individuals really contribute to their survival and chances of reproducing that same DNA. To repeat because it is so important, the DNA that has made it down the river of time is DNA that has, for hundreds of millions of years, inhabited the bodies of successful ancestors. Lots of would-be ancestors have died young, or failed to find a mate. But none of their DNA is still with us in the world.

It would be easy, at this point, to make the mistake of thinking that something, some elixir of success, some odour of sanctity from the good, successful, ancestral bodies 'rubs off' on the DNA as it passes through them. Nothing of the kind occurs. The river of DNA that flows through us into the future is a pure river that (mutations apart) leaves us exactly as it finds us. To be sure, it is continually mixed in sexual recombination. Half the DNA in you is from your father and the other half is from your mother. Each one of your sperms or eggs will contain a different mixture assembled from the genetic streamlet that came from your father and the genetic streamlet that came from your mother. But the point I was making remains true. Nothing about successful ancestors 'rubs off' on the genes as they pass through on their way to the distant future.

Accumulation of Luck

The Darwinian explanation for why living things are so good at doing what they do is very simple. They are good because of the accumulated wisdom of their ancestors. But it is not wisdom that they have learned or acquired. It is wisdom that they chanced upon by lucky random mutations, wisdom that was then selectively, nonrandomly, recorded in the genetic database of the species. In each generation the amount of luck was not very great: small enough to be believable even by the sceptical physicists whom I quoted earlier. But, because the luck has been accumulated over so many generations, we are eventually very impressed by the apparent improbability of the end product. The whole Darwinian circus depends upon—follows from—the existence of heredity. When I called heredity the basic ingredient, I meant that Darwinism, and hence life, will follow, more or less inevitably, on any planet in the universe where something equivalent to heredity arises.

We have arrived back at Mount Improbable, back to 'smearing out' the luck: to taking what looks like an immense amount of luck—the luck needed to make an eye where previously there was no eye, say—and explaining it by splitting it up into lots of little pieces of luck, each one added cumulatively to what has gone before. We have now seen how this actually works, by means of the accumulation of lots of little pieces of ancestral luck in the DNA that survives. Alongside the minority of genetically well-endowed individuals who survived, there were large numbers of less favoured individuals who perished. Every generation has its Darwinian failures but every individual is descended only from previous generations' successful minorities.

The message from the mountain is threefold. First is the message we have already introduced: there can be no sudden leaps upward—no precipitous increases in ordered complexity. Second, there can be no going downhill—species can't get worse as a prelude to getting better. Third, there may be more than one peak—more than one way of solving the same problem, all flourishing in the world.

How Early Bacteria Jump-Started Evolution

By Lynn Margulis and Dorion Sagan

When Charles Darwin published his theory of evolution in 1859, bacteria were a mystery. At virtually the same time in France, Louis Pasteur was conducting experiments that would eventually prove that bacteria were self-reproducing organisms, but their role in life's history would not be fully appreciated for a century. In the selection that follows, Lynn Margulis, a scientist who has done much to clarify our understanding of bacteria, and her son, Dorion Sagan, describe one of the crucial turns in life's history. Until 2 billion years ago, they write, the earth's atmosphere contained almost no oxygen, and its supply of carbon dioxide had been nearly depleted by microorganisms. This provoked a crisis for life, which depended on hydrogen-bearing compounds and carbon dioxide for its supply of fuel. Then a variety of blue-green bacteria evolved a new trick: They used light to split water molecules into their constituent atoms of hydrogen and oxygen. The hydrogen was used and the oxygen discarded, creating an oxygen-rich atmosphere. Eventually, oxygen-consuming organisms, the ancestors of all the plants and animals alive today, evolved. Lynn Margulis is Distinguished University Professor of Geosciences at the University of Massachusetts, Amherst. Dorion Sagan, whose father was the late astrophysicist Carl Sagan, is a science writer and magician.

The oxygen holocaust was a worldwide pollution crisis that occurred about 2,000 million years ago. Before this time there was almost no oxygen in the earth's atmosphere. The earth's original biosphere was as different from ours as that of an

Lynn Margulis and Dorion Sagan, *Microcosmos: Four Billion Years of Evolution from Our Microbial Ancestors*. New York: Summit Books, 1986. Copyright © 1986 by Lynn Margulis and Dorion Sagan. All rights reserved. Reproduced by permission.

alien planet. But purple and green photosynthetic microbes, frantic for hydrogen, discovered the ultimate resource, water, and its use led to the ultimate toxic waste, oxygen. Our precious oxygen was originally a gaseous poison dumped into the atmosphere. The appearance of oxygen-using photosynthesis and the resulting oxygen-rich environment tested the ingenuity of microbes, especially those producing oxygen and those nonmobile microorganisms unable to escape the newly abundant and reactive gas by means of motion. The microbes that stayed around responded by inventing various intracellular devices and scavengers to detoxify—and eventually exploit—the dangerous pollutant.

The unceasing demand for hydrogen initiated the crisis. Life's need for carbon-hydrogen compounds had already almost depleted carbon dioxide from the atmosphere. (The atmospheres of Mars and Venus today are still more than 95 percent carbon dioxide; the earth's is only 0.03 percent.) The lighter hydrogen gas kept escaping into space where it reacted with other elements, becoming ever less available. Even the earth's hydrogen sulfide, gurgling up through volcanoes, was becoming insufficient to supply the vast communities of photosynthetic bacteria that by the late Archean [Age] dominated the soils and waters.

Hydrogen from Water

But the earth was still full of an abundant hydrogen source: dihydrogen oxide, a.k.a. water. Until now, the strong bonds between the hydrogen and oxygen atoms in the water molecule (H_2O)— much stronger than those holding together the two hydrogens in hydrogen gas (H_2), hydrogen sulfide (H_2S), or organic molecules (CH_2O)—had been unbreakable by the resourceful, hydrogen-craving bacteria. Sometime after photosynthesis in the oxygen-poor atmosphere of the early earth had been well established, however, a kind of blue-green bacteria solved the hydrogen crisis forever. These were the ancestors to modern cyanobacteria.

The cyanobacterial ancestors seem to have been mutant sulfur bacteria desperate to continue living as their store of hydrogen sulfide dwindled. These organisms were already photosynthetic, and already had proteins inside them organized into so-called electron transport chains. In some of the blue-green bacteria, mutant DNA which coded for the electron transport chains duplicated. Experts at capturing sunlight in their reaction center to generate ATP, the new DNA led to the construction of a second photosynthetic reaction center. This second reaction center, by using light-generated electron energy from the first center, absorbed light again; but this was higher-energy light, absorbed at shorter wavelengths, that could split the water molecule into its hydrogen and oxygen constituents. The hydrogen was quickly grabbed and added onto carbon dioxide from the air to make organic food chemicals, such as sugars. In an evolutionary innovation unprecedented, as far as we know, in the universe, the blue-green alchemists, using light as energy, had extracted hydrogen from one of the planet's richest resources, water itself. This single metabolic change in tiny bacteria had major implications for the future history of all life on earth. . . .

Rising Oxygen Levels

For tens of millions of years excess oxygen [excreted by blue-green bacteria] was absorbed by live organisms, metal compounds, reduced atmospheric gases, and minerals in rocks. It began to accumulate in the atmosphere only by fits and starts. Many local populations were killed off, and many adaptations and protective devices evolved. From blue-green cyanobacteria that produced oxygen part-time emerged grass-green bacteria that emitted it continually. Thousands of species of aerobic photosynthesizers arose adapted to rocks, hot water locales, and scums. But by about 2,000 million years ago, the available passive reactants in the world had been used up and oxygen accumulated rapidly in the air, precipitating a catastrophe of global magnitude. People are gravely worried today about an increase in atmospheric carbon dioxide from 0.032 to 0.033 percent caused by our massive burning of fossil fuels. It is supposed that the "greenhouse effect" of the additional heat trapped by extra CO_2 could melt the ice caps, raising the level of the seas and flooding our urban coastlines, resulting in mass death and destruction. But the industrial pollution of our present, Phanerozoic Aeon is nothing compared to the strictly natural pollution of Archean and Proterozoic times. About 2,000 million years ago—give or take a couple of hundred million years—oxygen started rapidly increasing in our atmosphere. The Archeo-Proterozoic world saw an absolutely amazing increase in atmospheric oxygen from one part in a million to one part in five, from 0.0001 to 21 percent. This was by far the greatest pollution crisis the earth has ever endured.

Adapting to a New Atmosphere

Many kinds of microbes were immediately wiped out. Oxygen and light together are lethal—far more dangerous than either by itself. They are still instant killers of those anaerobes that survive in the airless nooks of the present world. When exposed to oxygen and light, the tissues of these unadapted organisms are instantly destroyed by subtle explosions. Microbial life had no defense against this cataclysm except the standard way of DNA replication and duplication, gene transfer, and mutation. From multiple deaths and an enhanced bacterial sexuality that is characteristic of bacteria exposed to toxins came a reorganization of the superorganism we [the authors] call the microcosm.

The newly resistant bacteria multiplied, and quickly replaced those sensitive to oxygen on the earth's surface as other bacteria survived beneath them in the anaerobic layers of mud and soil. From a holocaust that rivals the nuclear one we fear today [1986] came one of the most spectacular and important revolutions in the history of life.

From the earliest days of local oxygen exposure, gene duplication and transfer resulted in many protective mechanisms. The new genes were as important as survival manuals. The information they contained, so valuable to life on the newly oxygenic earth, spread through the reorganizing microcosm. Bioluminescence and the synthesis of vitamin E are some of the innovations scientists surmise arose in response to the oxygen threat. But adaptation didn't stop there. In one of the greatest coups of all time, the cyanobacteria invented a metabolic system that *required* the very substance that had been a deadly poison.

Oxygen as Fuel

Aerobic respiration, the breathing of oxygen, is an ingeniously efficient way of channeling and exploiting the reactivity of oxygen. It is essentially controlled combustion that breaks down organic molecules and yields carbon dioxide, water, and a great deal of energy into the bargain. Whereas fermentation typically produces two molecules of ATP from every sugar molecule broken down, the respiration of the same sugar molecule utilizing oxygen can produce as many as thirty-six. Pushed—not, probably, to its breaking point, but to a point of intense global stress—the microcosm did more than adapt: it evolved an oxygen-using dynamo that changed life and its terrestrial dwelling place forever.

Some cyanobacteria respire only in the dark—apparently because they use some of the same molecular machinery for both their respiratory and their photosynthetic electron transport chains. The shared parts can't be used simultaneously for both pathways. (Algae and plants both respire and photosynthesize) because the two processes take place in different parts of the cell: photosynthesis in the chloroplasts and respiration in the mitochondria. . . .

Cyanobacteria now had both photosynthesis which generated oxygen and respiration which consumed it. They had found their place in the sun. Given only sunlight, a few salts always present in natural waters, and atmospheric carbon dioxide, they could make everything they needed: nucleic acids, proteins, vitamins, and the machinery for making them. If biosynthetic ability alone were considered a measure of evolutionary advancement, we humans would be far behind the cyanobacteria. Our complicated nutritional requirements leave us utterly dependent on plants and microbes to supply what we cannot make for ourselves. We are, in a very real sense, parasites of the microcosm.

Rapid Diversification

Not surprisingly, with the greater quantities of energy available to them, cyanobacteria exploded into hundreds of different forms, tiny (most only a few micrometers in diameter) and large (80 micrometers or eight percent of a millimeter). They made simple spheres embedded in a gelatinous matrix of sheets of many cells, elaborately branched filaments that could release wet spores from their tips, and cells containing special oxygen-proof cysts that carried on anaerobic nitrogen fixation.

They spread into greater extremes of the environment, from cold marine waters to hot freshwater springs. New food relationships developed as other bacteria fed off cyanobacterial starch, sugar, small metabolites, and even the fixed carbon and nitrogen of their dead bodies. But most significant, cyanobacteria's continuing air pollution forced other organisms to acquire the ability to use oxygen, too. This set off waves of speciation and the creation of elaborate forms and life cycles among them.

The stabilization of atmospheric oxygen at about 21 percent seems to be a mute consensus reached by the biota millions of years ago; indeed it is a contract still respected today. If the oxygen concentration had ever risen much higher than this, the fossil record certainly would reveal evidence of worldwide conflagration. The present high, but not too high, level of oxygen in our atmosphere gives the impression of a conscious decision to maintain balance between danger and opportunity, between risk and benefit. Even the rain forests and grasslands are extremely flammable when water levels are low. If oxygen were a few percent higher, living organisms themselves would spontaneously combust. As oxygen falls a few percent aerobic organisms start to asphyxiate. The biosphere has maintained this happy medium for hundreds of millions of years at least. While just how this works is still a mystery . . . worldwide regulatory mechanisms controlling temperature and gas composition can hypothetically arise from the normal growth properties of organisms. The leveling off and subsequent continuous modulation of the quantities of oxygen in the atmosphere was an event as welcome as the holocaust was terrible. One way of putting it is that, assuming life halted the oxygen build-up, it must have developed tremendous knowledge of antipollution engineering systems. The alternative perspective is that the cybernetic control of the earth's surface by unintelligent organisms calls into question the supposed uniqueness of human consciousness. Microbes apparently did not plan to bring under control a pollution crisis of amazingly daunting proportions. Yet they did what no governmental agency or bureaucracy on earth today could ever do. Growing, mutating, and trading genes, some bacteria producing oxygen and others removing it, they maintained the oxygen balance of an entire planet. . . .

The Basis of Complex Life

As soon as there were significant quantities of oxygen in the air an ozone shield built up. It formed in the stratosphere, floating on top of the rest of the air. This layer of three-atom oxygen molecules put a final stop to the abiotic synthesis of organic compounds by screening out the high-energy ultraviolet rays.

The production of food and oxygen from light were to make microbes the basis of a global food cycle that extends to us today; animals could never have evolved without the food of photosynthesis and the oxygen in the air. The energy dynamo created by cyanobacterial pollution was a prerequisite for a new unit of life—

the nucleated cell which is the fundamental component of plant, animal, protist, and fungal life. In eukaryotes, genes are packaged in a nucleus and there is an elaborate orchestration of internal cell processes, including the presence in the area surrounding the nucleus (the cytoplasm) of mitochondria—special structures that metabolize oxygen for the rest of the cell. So different is the organization of the eukaryotic from the prokaryotic or bacterial cell that the two types represent the most fundamental separation among known life forms. Perhaps their origin in the midst of the extreme selection pressures of the oxygen catastrophe made eukaryotic cells so different. But the difference between nonnucleated bacterial cells and cells with nuclei is far greater than that between plants and animals.

Before cyanobacteria split water molecules and produced oxygen, there was no indication that the earth's patina of life would ever be more than an inconspicuous scum lying on the ground. That it did develop and expand into gardens and jungles and cities is testimony to the power of microbial mats and seaside slime to alter each other in their local habitats. But the microbes created an even greater impact. They altered the entire surface of the earth. The biosphere, humming with the thrill and danger of free oxygen, eventually emerged from the crisis. But the earth was a changed place. It had become a planetary anomaly.

By the middle of the Proterozoic Aeon 1,500 million years ago most of biochemical evolution had been accomplished. The earth's modern surface and atmosphere were largely established. Microbial life permeated the air, soil, and water, cycling gases and other elements through the earth's fluids as they do today. With the exception of a few exotic compounds, such as the essential oils and hallucinogens of flowering plants and the exquisitely effective snake venoms, prokaryotic microbes can assemble and disassemble all the molecules of modern life.

Transformation Accomplished

Judging from the perspective of the planetwide accomplishments of early life, it is not surprising that the development of life's biochemical repertoire occurred over a full two billion years. The microbial stage lasted nearly twice as long as the rest of evolution to the present day. As Abraham Lincoln is reported to have said, "If I had eight hours to chop down a tree, I'd spend six sharpening my ax." The microcosm did just that. It set the stage for the respective evolutions of fungi, animals, and plants, all of which arose in relatively rapid succession. Just as in psychology, where the early years of infancy and childhood are known to be crucial to the development of adult personality, the early aeons of life defined the contours of modern living. The Age of Bacteria transformed the earth from a cratered moonlike terrain of volcanic glassy rocks into the fertile planet in which we make our home. The alien primeval world lacking an atmosphere of oxygen was to be no more. Unlike neighboring Mars and Venus, whose atmospheres settled down to become stable chemical mixtures of carbon dioxide, the earth had gotten energized. Delivered from the mercy of time, it became engulfed in the creative, autopoietic processes of life.

Tracing Humanity's Origins

By Richard Leakey and Roger Lewin

The evolution of humans has long been a subject of fascination and controversy. The fossil record did not yield a clear picture for many years, and hoaxes, errors, and prejudice further confused the scientific literature. Beginning in the 1950s, however, a stream of fossil evidence out of Africa began to clarify the picture. No one contributed more to that evidence than the Leakey family. In the selection that follows, Richard Leakey, a second-generation scion of the naturalist family, reviews evidence indicating that human ancestors branched off some 7 million years ago from one of various species of apes living in Africa. He and coauthor Roger Lewin contend that human ancestors developed bipedalism—walking upright on two legs—in response to environmental changes. As forest cover became spotty, bipedalism gave human ancestors an efficient way to walk from grove to grove while retaining the ability to climb trees in search of food or shelter. That advantage, they suggest, was enough to launch bipedal apes on an evolutionary course that led, eventually, to modern humans. Thus, they conclude, humans are a variety of ape, though a rather special one. Leakey is one of the world's leading paleoanthropologists. He heads Kenya's Wildlife Service. Coauthor Roger Lewin is an accomplished science writer.

For me, the fundamental distinction between us and our closest relatives is not our language, not our culture, not our technology. It is that we stand upright, with our lower limbs for support and locomotion and our upper limbs free from those functions. In essence, humans are bipedal apes who happened to develop all these other qualities we usually associate with being human. And if we think again about the molecular data, which ally us closely with the chimpanzee and gorilla, then, no question about it, we are apes of a kind, "rather odd African apes," as David Pilbeam once put it.

The prehistoric record in Africa is now extensive, no longer the quip about fewer fossils than would cover a dining room table. By my count there are fossilized fragments of about a thousand human individuals from the early part of our evolution, and I wouldn't even try to count the number of stone tools. All this shows clearly that the earliest stone tools appear in the record about 2.5 million years ago, some five million years after the origin of the human family. Of one thing we can therefore be certain: the Darwinian package of bipedalism, tool making, and intelligence marching in evolutionary concert is not correct.

So important to our later evolutionary history was the freeing of our hands that my preference is to use the term "human" for the first bipedal apes. I know that many people become exercised about the implications of names, particularly when it comes to us, but for me, "human" and "bipedal ape" are synonymous. I'm not saying that once the bipedal ape had evolved, you and I were evolutionary inevitabilities, because evolution doesn't work like that. Nor am I suggesting that the earliest bipedal apes had the same intellectual powers or outlook as we do. Of course they didn't. All I am suggesting is that the origin of a bipedal form of locomotion was so fundamental a change, so replete with profound evolutionary potential, that we should recognize the roots of our humanity where they really are. I would make a distinction, however, between calling the first bipedal apes human and expecting to find humanlike behavior in these creatures. Once we recognize the importance in our history of the origin of bipedalism, we can begin to identify the emergence through evolutionary time of that intangible, indefinable, and yet intensely felt sense in us that we identify as true humanity. . . .

Upstarts Among the Apes

By about ten million years ago, with the new topography of the eastern part of the continent [Africa] still building, there was a great diversity of ape species, something of which we are only now becoming aware. Now there are only three ape species in Africa— the common chimpanzee, the pygmy chimpanzee, and the gorilla. Back then, there were as many as twenty. Between ten million and five million years ago, that wonderful diversity began to decline, in part because of competition from a rising number of Old World monkey species, and in part because of the changing habitat. One of the ape species underwent the dramatic evolutionary transformation to become the first bipedal ape, which, as far as we know, was the only time this mode of locomotion had evolved among primates. As a result, while diversity of most ape groups was declining, among the bipedal apes it suddenly burgeoned. A new evolutionary group began to grow, variations on an evolutionary novelty. The immediate question is how this new diversity of bipedal apes thrived where other apes apparently could not.

We have already dismissed the beginnings of stone tool making as the provider of that evolutionary edge: it appeared far too late in our family's history to have been important in the establishment of the family. And the transformation into a hunting ape can equally be set aside as an explanation, for the same reason. A very "human-oriented" explanation, the hunting ape hypothesis finds no support in the archeological evidence, which indicates that hunting became important in the human career relatively late, beginning, probably, with the *Homo* lineage. No, to discover the nature of that evolutionary edge we have to look for more basic reasons, basic biology, not aspects of human culture. Of the hypotheses advanced in recent years in this category, two seem to me to be interesting. One was proposed by Owen Lovejoy, the other by Peter Rodman and Henry McHenry of the University of California at Davis. Lovejoy's hypothesis enjoyed a blaze of publicity. Rodman and McHenry's did not. It is easy to see why.

Freeing Hands to Carry

Lovejoy is a fine anatomist, a specialist in the mechanics and origin of bipedalism. He decided some years ago to see whether the biological differences between apes and humans may have provided a competitive edge for the development of upright locomotion. His opening premise was very direct: "Hominids became bipeds for some specific biological reason," he explained recently. "It wasn't for locomotion, because bipedalism is a lousy way of getting around. It must have been for carrying things." As bipeds, humans are embarrassingly slow on foot and not particularly agile in the trees. It is also true that the hands, freed from locomotor duties, could carry things. There are two ways to view this, of course. First, that hominids became bipedal *in order to* free the hands for carrying things. Second, that in becoming bipedal for some other reason, hominids were *able* to carry things. Lovejoy prefers the first of these two views.

Another part of Lovejoy's argument is that, because so drastic an anatomical rebuilding is required to transform a quadruped into a biped, an animal in which the evolutionary change is still incomplete would be an inefficient biped. "During this period, a reproductive advantage must have fallen to those in each generation that walked more frequently in bipedal posture *despite* their lack of efficiency," he reasoned. "When a trait proves to have so powerful a selective advantage, it almost always has some direct bearing on the rate of reproduction. But how could our ancestors have had more successful offspring by walking upright?"

The subsequent argument runs something like this. Apes reproduce slowly, with births spaced widely apart, once every four years. If the bipedal ape could increase its reproductive output, producing infants more frequently, it would be at an overall selective advantage. Because much of biology is driven by energy supply, an increased reproductive output would require greater energy in the female. How was she to achieve this? "Males represent an untapped pool of reproductive energy," concluded Lovejoy. "If a male provisions a female with food, the female has more energy available for parenting, and more offspring can be produced." In order to provision a female, a male must be able to gather food and bring it back to her. Hence the need to walk bipedally, freeing the hands to carry things.

But there is more to it than that. Lovejoy's hypothesis seems to explain everything, perhaps too much. For instance, a male would be foolish to provision a female unless he was sure that her offspring were his. There is no genetic advantage to be had by a male if he helps to rear the offspring of another male. A bond between male and female must develop, in which the female stops publicly advertising sexual readiness but remains constantly attractive to her mate. . . .

Problems Arise

Lovejoy points out that in such [monogamous] pairs there is little or no difference in the size of canine teeth—there is no canine dimorphism. But it is also true that in monogamous pairs there usually is little difference in male and female size—no body-size dimorphism. And yet one of the things we can infer from the earliest human fossils is that there was considerable body-size dimorphism: males were about twice the size of females, a difference we see in modern gorillas. The body-size dimorphism in primates is always associated with competition among males for access to females, and some kind of polygyny, with one male controlling sexual access to several females. It never occurs in monogamous species, where one male has access to only one female. So, although Lovejoy's hypothesis is attractive, it seems to trip over the very rules of biology that inspired it. I applaud the attempt, but I think it fails.

Upright Efficiency

The second biology-based hypothesis for the origin of bipedalism is very different from Lovejoy's. For a start, it focuses on locomotion, not the ability to carry things, as the immediate benefit. And it explains only bipedalism, not a whole host of other human characteristics. In this hypothesis, the freeing of the hands is a consequence, not a cause, of bipedalism.

Peter Rodman is a primatologist and Henry McHenry is an anthropologist. Their offices are separated by a few steps along the corridor in the main biology building at the Davis campus. They decided to look at bipedalism from the viewpoint of an ape, asking what it could and could not do. And they rounded up some data on the energetics of walking, in humans and apes, work that had been done some years earlier by researchers at Harvard. "We looked at the data and saw that, for a chimpanzee, walking quadrupedally was no more and no less energetically expensive than walking bipedally," explains Rodman. "So if you imagine that hominids evolved from some kind of quadrupedal ape, then you see that there's no energy barrier, no energy Rubicon in going from quadrupedalism to bipedalism. But the most important point—a new one, as far as we know—is that bipedalism in humans is considerably more efficient than quadrupedalism in living apes.". . .

Chimpanzees are not particularly good quadrupeds energetically, especially over long distances, because their style of locomotion is a compromise between walking on the ground and climbing in the trees.

"If you're an ape, and you find yourself in ecological circumstances where a more efficient mode of locomotion would be advantageous, the evolution of bipedalism is a likely outcome," says Rodman. "What kind of ecological circumstance might that be?" Rodman and McHenry point to the fragmentation of forest cover occurring east of the [African] Rift Valley ten million years ago. As time went on, "food was more dispersed and demanded more travel to harvest." In other words, there was no change in diet other than that the food itself—on trees and bushes—was widely scattered in open woodland rather than densely packed as in the original forest cover. "Bipedalism provided the possibility of improved efficiency of travel with modification only of hind limbs while leaving the [ape] structure of the forelimbs free for arboreal feeding." So, they conclude, "the primary adaptation of the Hominidae is an ape's way of living where an ape could not live."

An Ape Who Stood Tall

If true, it means that the first human was indeed simply a bipedal ape. The changes in teeth and jaw structure that we associate with human fossils may have developed later as further environmental change encouraged a gradual shift in diet. We can never be sure, of course, which hypothesis is correct, because, as with all of evolution, we are dealing with a singular historic event. We have to make judgments on what appears to be the most scientifically persuasive. To me, Rodman and McHenry's hypothesis is one of the most persuasive we have. As [primatologist] Sarah Hrdy observes, "Rodman and McHenry's hypothesis is practical, scarcely the stuff of myths."

I said earlier that the fundamental distinction between humans and apes is that we stand upright, with our upper limbs free. And yet I have suggested that the first human was a bipedal ape. Although this may seem contradictory, it is not. The two statements are based on different perspectives: one, that of history as we know it to have unfolded, the second, that of the biology of the first human. Unless our ancestors had upper limbs free from locomotion, they would not have been able to evolve many of the capabilities that contributed to our humanity, such as the elaboration of material culture within a social context. But the first human species can best be described as a bipedal ape.

In the larger sweep of history, we can look at the changing climate from ten million years ago onward; we can look at the geological stirrings that altered the topography and vegetation patterns of East Africa; and we can say, yes, the first human evolved as a direct response to those changes. The environmental circumstances were favorable for the evolution of bipedalism in a quadrupedal ancestor, the consequences of natural selection. I know that many people would prefer to imagine a more significant beginning to the human family, something a little more awe-inspiring. This sentiment was part of the inspiration of the long-popular myth of the intrepid ape striding out into the savannah, there to triumph over adverse circumstances.

It is also true that some of us believe the very fact of being bipedal somehow bestowed a nobility upon the first human species. By being bipedal, our earliest ancestors undoubtedly gained certain practical benefits, such as the ability to carry things and habitually to have a better view across the terrain. But to assume that they were consequently noble is to view the posture through our own experience as fully modern humans, creatures who have come to dominate the world in so many ways. Having experienced what it is to be human in the fullest sense, we find it difficult, perhaps impossible, to view the world through the eyes of creatures different from ourselves, through the eyes of the first bipedal ape. . . .

Genetic Relations

It turns out that the difference between us, in the basic genetic blueprint, DNA, is less than 2 percent. This is smaller than the genetic difference between a horse and a zebra, which are capable of mating and producing offspring, albeit infertile offspring. There has long been speculation on the possible outcome of sexual union between humans and chimpanzees, fueled in the early years of anthropology by the erroneous notion that apes were a form of regressed humankind. Even in these days of genetic sophistication there are persistent—and always unconfirmed—rumors of "experimental" matings between humans and chimpanzees. As it happens, even though the genetic blueprints of humans and chimpanzees are similar, at some point in human history a change occurred in the packaging of the DNA. The DNA of apes is packaged in 24 pairs of chromosomes, in humans, in 23 pairs, a difference that would probably make barren any such sexual union.

The degree of genetic difference between humans and the African apes is of the magnitude that geneticists usually associate with closely associated, or sister, species. For instance, horses and zebras are placed in the same genus, *Equus*. Yet anthropologists have traditionally placed humans and apes in separate biological families, which implies a big difference indeed. No wonder Morris Goodman wanted to change things in 1962, when he said that humans and apes should be classified within the same biological family.

And now he has a bigger reason than ever to change things, because molecular evidence has just produced potentially the biggest surprise of all. Until recently, the molecular data seemed to indicate that humans were about equally distant genetically from chimpanzees and from gorillas. Chimps and gorillas could be imagined as having split off from the last common ancestor at about the same time, producing the African apes as one group and humans as a second group.

Closest to Chimps

Now, however, more molecular evidence indicates that gorillas may have diverged from the common stock as much as two million years earlier than chimpanzees, some 9.5 million years ago. Chimpanzees and humans separated from each other about 7.5 million years ago. This leaves us with the startling conclusion that the chimp is more closely related to us than it is to the gorilla. Goodman and his colleagues base their conclusion on comparisons of the actual structure—the DNA sequence—of important genes in humans and apes. It is molecular anthropology at its most exquisitely detailed.

"If Morris Goodman is correct in his conclusion, we will just have to go back to the anatomical evidence and find out what we've been missing," says Lawrence Martin, an anthropologist at the State University of New York at Stony Brook. Martin's concern—the concern for many of us—is that chimpanzees and gorillas are similar anatomically, including their unique mode of locomotion, knuckle walking. Knuckle walkers use bent fingers, not the flat of the hand, to support their weight on their forelimbs. "If chimps and gorillas arose separately, it would mean that their similar anatomy, including the knuckle-walking complex, must have evolved independently," says Martin. "Anything is possible theoretically, but it doesn't seem likely."

Martin has recently completed a detailed study of key anatomical features in chimpanzees, gorillas, and humans, looking for signs of relatedness. Jointly with Peter Andrews, a colleague from the Natural History Museum in London, he concludes that, although the three form a natural biological group, the chimpanzee and gorilla are each other's closest relative, with humans slightly more distant. . . .

Knuckle-Walking Ancestors

Let us suppose for a moment that this latest conclusion from molecular biology is correct—and, incidentally, it is not unanimously supported by geneticists. Does it have any implications, other than that we are even more intimately in the camp of the African apes than we imagined? "It means that it is more likely than not that the immediate ancestor to humans was a knuckle walker," suggests David Pilbeam. This addresses Martin's comment about the probability that knuckle walking evolved twice. "It's more parsimonious to assume that knuckle walking evolved once only, and was part of the ancestral condition from which first gorillas and then chimpanzees and humans evolved," David replies. "In that case, the African apes maintained this ancestral mode of locomotion, and humans changed theirs."

Does this mean that Sherwood Washburn was right all along, when he suggested in the 1960s that our ancestors were knuckle walkers? I can't be certain one way or the other, but I do know that in the earliest human fossils that could bear vestigial traces of knuckle walking—the four-million-year-old arm bones from east Lake Turkana—there is no sign of knuckle walking. There are strong indications in the wrist's anatomy of an adaptation to tree climbing, but not to knuckle walking. Perhaps all vestiges were lost in the time between the origin of hominids and the life of this individual, a gap of some 2.5 million years, certainly long enough for a great deal of anatomical evolution. We don't know. We will only know when we find evidence of the very first bipedal apes. And that, I hope, will be soon.

Whether Goodman and his colleagues are correct in believing the chimpanzee to be our first cousin and the gorilla a more distant second cousin, there is no longer any doubt about our proper place in nature: we are an ape of a rather unusual kind. And Goodman is certainly correct to suggest revision at last of the formal biological classification: the two knuckle walkers and the bipedal ape belong in one family, African apes all.

CHAPTER 3

Contemporary Controversies

Evolution Is Unscientific

By Duane Gish

There are two general theories of life's history, says creationist and biochemist Duane Gish in the following selection. One is the evolutionary model, which he notes most scientists accept; the other is the creation model, which involves a supernatural power (usually considered to be God) designing and creating every form of life. Gish claims that evolution does not meet the criteria to be considered a scientific theory, which requires that postulates be observable and testable. First, he claims that evolution has never been observed. He also contends that no experiment can conceivably falsify the theory. Gish quotes various scientists in support of his argument that evolution is unobservable and untestable. Duane Gish holds a doctorate in biochemistry from the University of California at Berkeley. He serves as senior vice president of the Institute for Creation Research, a California-based organization that describes itself as "a Christ-focused Creation ministry where science and the Bible are fully integrated."

The proponents of evolution theory adamantly insist that special creation be excluded from any possible consideration as an explanation for origins on the basis that it does not qualify as a scientific theory. On the other hand, they would view as unthinkable the consideration of evolution as anything less than pure science. In fact, . . . most evolutionists insist that evolution must no longer be thought of as a theory, but must be considered to be a fact. However, evolution does not even qualify as a scientific theory, according to a strict definition of the latter.

What criteria must be met for a theory to be considered as scientific in the usually accepted sense? George Gaylord Simpson

has stated that "it is inherent in any definition of science that statements that cannot be checked by observation are not really about
anything . . . or at the very least, they are not science." A definition of science given by the Oxford Dictionary is:

> A branch of study which is concerned either with a connected
> body of *demonstrated truths* or with *observed fact* systematically
> classified and more or less colligated by being brought under gen-
> eral laws, and which includes trustworthy methods for the dis-
> covery of new truth within its own domain. (Emphasis added.)

Thus, for a theory to qualify as a scientific theory, it must be
supported by events, processes, or properties which can be re-
peatedly observed, and the theory must be useful in predicting the
outcome of future natural phenomena or laboratory experiments.
An additional limitation usually imposed is that the theory must
be capable of falsification. That is, it must be possible to conceive
some experiment, the failure of which would disprove the theory.

It is on the basis of such criteria that most evolutionists insist that
creation be refused consideration as a possible explanation for origins. Creation has not been witnessed by human observers, it cannot be tested experimentally, and as a theory it is nonfalsifiable.

An Unobserved Phenomenon

The general theory of evolution also fails to meet all three of these
criteria, however. It is obvious, for example, that there were no human observers to the origin of the universe, the origin of life, the
conversion of a fish into an amphibian, or an ape into a man. No
one, as a matter of fact, has ever observed the origin of a species
by naturally occurring processes. Evolution has been *postulated*,
but it has never been *observed*. . . .

It can be seen that evolutionists seek to excuse the fact that evolution cannot be observed or tested experimentally on the basis
that real evolutionary events require great lengths of time for their
consummation. Yes, it is true that the evolutionary process postulated would require more time than we have available for human
observation. But then, it is obvious that evolution can never be
more than just a postulate.

[Lawyer Norman] Macbeth, who was by no means a creationist, has flatly stated that "Darwinism is not science." [L.C.] Birch

and [P.R.] Ehrlich state that the theory of evolution "is 'outside of empirical science' but not necessarily false. No one can think of ways in which to test it."

After stating that the neo-Darwinian theory of evolution is based on axioms (concepts that can be neither proved nor tested), evolution theorist [C. Leon] Harris proclaims:

> The axiomatic nature of the neo-Darwinian theory places the debate between evolutionists and creationists in a new perspective. Evolutionists have often challenged creationists to provide experimental proof that species have been fashioned *de novo*. Creationists have often demanded that evolutionists show how chance mutations can lead to adaptability, or to explain why natural selection has favored some species but not others with special adaptations, or why natural selection allows apparently detrimental organs to persist. We may now recognize that neither challenge is fair. If the neo-Darwinian theory is axiomatic, it is not valid for creationists to demand proof of the axioms, and it is not valid for evolutionists to dismiss special creation as unproved so long as it is stated as an axiom. . . .

Growing Doubts

More and more evolutionists have come to doubt the modern neo-Darwinian theory of evolution so prevalent today. They realize that the fossil record does not produce the evidence of gradual change demanded by Darwinism and they have sought to devise new ideas about the mechanism of evolution. This has generated fierce opposition from the old guard, the defenders of neo-Darwinism, and intense controversy within evolutionary circles has resulted. This fact was revealed in the article, "Science Contra Darwin" by Sharon Begley, which appeared in *Newsweek*. She states:

> The great body of work derived from Charles Darwin's revolutionary 1859 book, *On the Origin of Species*, is under increasing attack—and not just from creationists. . . . So heated is the debate that one Darwinian says there are times when he thinks about going into a field with more intellectual honesty: the used-car business.

[Biochemist] Michael Denton is neither a Christian nor a professing creationist. He holds both an M.D. and a Ph.D. from British universities. No one can accuse him of being a fundamentalist out on the lunatic fringe. Nevertheless, he has published a devastating critique of modern evolutionary theory. On every count, according to Dr. Denton, evolution strikes out. His book is one of the most incisive, thoroughly documented, and comprehensive books that describes the vast amount of scientific evidence that refutes evolutionary theory. On the flap of the book published in 1985 are recorded the following comments:

> The theory of evolution, as propounded by Darwin and elaborated into accepted "fact" by biologists, is in serious trouble. This sober, authoritative, and responsible book by a practicing scientist presents an accurate account of the rapidly accumulating evidence which threatens to destroy almost every cherished tenet of Darwinian evolution. Although the theory has proved to be right about the relatively minor phenomenon of speciation, its larger claims to account for the relationship between the classes and orders, let alone the origin of life, appear to be based on very shaky scientific foundations indeed. Not only has paleontology failed spectacularly to come up with the fossil "missing links" which Darwin anticipated, but hypothetical reconstructions of major evolutionary developments—such as that linking birds to reptiles—are beginning to look more and more like science fiction fantasies than serious conjectures. Even the currently fashionable theory of "punctuated equilibrium" cannot adequately fill in the very real gaps we face when envisaging how major groups of plants and animals arose.

Molecular Findings

> Most important of all, the discoveries of molecular biologists, of whom Michael Denton is one, far from strengthening Darwinian claims, are throwing more and more doubt upon the correctness of the whole theory. When the amino acid sequences, the basic evidence of a cell's hereditary antecedents, of supposedly related species are examined the results point, not towards the Darwinian picture of a nature linked by the genetic descent of one class from another, but towards the typological model of nature which Darwinism usurped. At a fundamental level of molecular structure, each member of a class seems equally representative of that class and no species appears to be in any real sense "intermediate" between two classes. Nature, in short, appears to be profoundly discontinuous. Furthermore, advances in biochemistry are making the existence of

a "prebiotic soup"—the supposed primordial broth in which life began on Earth—look highly unlikely if not completely absurd.

Darwinism Termed Myth

Søren Løvtrup is a well-known Swedish biologist. He is a totally committed evolutionist, but nevertheless he completely rejects the neo-Darwinian theory of evolution. He maintains that mutations and natural selection have had little, if anything, to do with evolution. He is an advocate of the view that macromutations, generating large jumps in evolution, provided the mechanism of evolution. He refers to the modern neo-Darwinian theory of evolution, the theory that is currently being taught as dogma in practically all of the textbooks in use in secondary schools, colleges, and universities in the U.S., as the "Darwinian myth." In 1987 he published a book entitled *Darwinism: The Refutation of a Myth*. In this book Løvtrup reviews the history of Darwinism from its beginning up to its present-day formulation. He describes his objections to the theory, and presents his own ideas about evolutionary theory. Among his conclusions we find the following statements:

> I suppose that nobody will deny that it is a great misfortune if an entire branch of science becomes addicted to a false theory. But this is what has happened in biology: for a long time now people discuss evolutionary problems in a peculiar "Darwinian" vocabulary— "adaptation," "selection pressure," "natural selection," etc.—thereby believing that they contribute to the *explanation* of natural events. They do not, and the sooner this is discovered, the sooner we shall be able to make real progress in our understanding of evolution.
>
> *I believe that one day the Darwinian myth will be ranked the greatest deceit in the history of science.* (Emphasis added.)

What an astounding situation! What is being taught in our schools and universities as established truth, a dogma not to be questioned, Løvtrup denounces as the greatest deceit ever perpetuated in the history of science! Creation scientists maintain that not only is modern Darwinian theory the greatest deceit in the history of science, but the very notion of evolution itself is the greatest deceit ever to gain currency in scientific circles. Not that evolutionists are deliberately dishonest, but they have been deceived or have deceived themselves to believe something that is totally false.

In view of the above, it is incredible that most leading scientists dogmatically insist that the molecule-to-man evolution theory be taught as a fact to the exclusion of all other postulates. Evolution in this broad sense is unproven and unprovable and thus cannot be considered as fact. It is not subject to test by the ordinary methods of experimental science—observation and falsification. It thus does not, in a strict sense, even qualify as a scientific theory. It is a postulate and may serve as a model within which attempts may be made to explain and correlate the evidence from the historical record, that is, the fossil record, and to make predictions concerning the nature of future discoveries.

Evolutionists, however, insist that evolution is fact, not theory. Philosopher Tom Bethell describes the true situation when he states:

> Evolution is perhaps the most jealously guarded dogma of the American public philosophy. Any sign of serious resistance to it has encountered fierce hostility in the past, and it will not be abandoned without a tremendous fight. The gold standard could go (glad to be rid of that!), Saigon abandoned, the Constitution itself slyly junked. But Darwinism will be defended to the bitter end.

Creationism as Scientific Model

Creation is, of course, unproven and unprovable and thus cannot be considered as fact. It is not subject to test by the ordinary methods of experimental science—observation and falsification. It thus does not, in a strict sense, qualify as a scientific theory. It is a postulate and may serve as a model within which attempts may be made to explain and correlate the evidence from the historical record, that is, the fossil record, and to make predictions concerning the nature of future discoveries. . . .

The Creation Research Society, an organization of Christian men and women of science, all of whom hold advanced degrees and are fully committed to the acceptance of creation as opposed to evolution, now numbers about 600 in membership. There is yet a vastly larger number of scientists who do not accept the theory but choose to remain silent for a variety of reasons.

Why have most scientists accepted the theory of evolution? Is the evidence really that convincing? This seems to be the clear implication. On the other hand, is it possible that that many scientists could be wrong? The answer is an emphatic "YES!" Consider for a moment some historical examples. For centuries the accepted scientific view was that all planets revolved around the earth. This was the Ptolemaic geocentric theory of the universe. Only after a prolonged and bitter controversy did the efforts of Copernicus, Galileo, and others succeed in convincing the scientific world that the Ptolemaic system was wrong and that Copernicus was right in his contention that the planets in the solar system revolved around the sun.

At one time most people with scientific training who rejected creation accepted as fact the idea that life spontaneously arose from nonlife. Thus, frogs supposedly spontaneously arose from swamps, decaying matter generated flies, and rats were brought to life out of matter found in debris, etc. A series of carefully designed and executed experiments by [Francesco] Redi, [Lazzaro] Spallanzani, and [Louis] Pasteur spanning 200 years were required to put to rest the theory of the spontaneous generation of life.

In recent times, a theory dealing with weak interaction of atomic particles became so widely accepted by physicists that it won the status of a law, the Law of Parity. During the 1950s, two brilliant Chinese-American scientists performed a series of experiments that disproved the theory and deposed the "Law."

In all of the above examples, the vast majority of scientists were wrong and a small minority were right. No doubt, strong preconceived ideas and prejudices were powerful factors in accounting for the fact that scientists were reluctant to give up the geocentric theory of the universe and the theory of the spontaneous generation of life.

Prejudice Behind Evolution

The effects of prejudice and preconceived ideas are of overwhelming importance in the acceptance of the theory of evolution. The reason most scientists accept evolution has nothing to do, primarily, with the evidence. The reason that most scientists accept the theory of evolution is that most scientists are unbelievers, and unbelieving, materialistic individuals are forced to accept a materialistic, naturalistic explanation for the origin of all living things. [Zoologist David M.S.] Watson, for example, has referred to the theory of evolution as "a theory universally accepted not because it can be proved by logically coherent evidence to be true, but because the only alternative, special creation, is clearly incredible.". . .

No doubt a large majority of the scientific community embraces the mechanistic materialistic philosophy of [evolutionists George] Simpson, [Julian] Huxley, [Jacques] Monod, and Darwinists in general. Many of these men are highly intelligent, and they have woven the fabric of evolution theory in an ingenious fashion. They have then combined this evolution theory with humanistic philosophy and have clothed the whole with the term, "science." The product, a nontheistic religion, with evolutionary philosophy as its creed under the guise of "science," is being taught in most public schools, colleges, and universities of the United States. It has become our unofficial state-sanctioned religion.

Contrary to the Bible

The evolutionist's view of man as expressed by Simpson and Huxley is in direct contrast to the Biblical view of man, found, for example, in Psalm 100, verse 3: "Know ye that the Lord He is God: it is He that hath made us and not we ourselves; we are His people and the sheep of His pasture." The Bible does indeed reveal that there is a living God who has created us and who controls our destiny.

Furthermore, a God who is great enough to create and control this universe is great enough, once having given His revelation to man, to preserve that revelation free from error. This preservation was not dependent upon man, but succeeded in spite of man. In this revelation, found in the first two chapters of Genesis in the Bible, the account of creation is recorded in a grand but concise fashion.

Not all evolutionists are materialistic atheists or agnostics. Many evolutionists believe in God, and some even believe the Bible to be the Word of God. They believe that evolution was God's method of creation, that God initiated the process at the molecular level and then allowed it to follow its natural course. The Biblical and scientific evidence, however, tells just as strongly against theistic evolution as it does against any other form of evolution.

The first two chapters of Genesis were not written in the form of parables or poetry, but present the broad outlines of creation in the form of simple historical facts. These facts directly contradict evolution theory. The Bible tells us that at one time in history there was a single human being upon the earth—a male by the name of Adam. This is in basic contradiction to evolution theory, because, according to that theory, populations evolve, not individuals. After God had formed Adam from the dust of the ground, the Bible tells us that He used some portion from Adam's side (in the King James Version, this is translated as "rib") to form Eve. This, of course, cannot be reconciled with any possible evolutionary theory concerning the origin of man.

The New Testament Scriptures fully support this Genesis account. For example, in I Corinthians 11:8 we read, "Man is not of the woman, but the woman of the man." By any natural reproductive process, man is always born of a woman. We all have mothers. This Biblical account can, therefore, be referring only to that unique time in history when God created woman from man, just as described in Genesis 2:21, 22.

It is apparent that acceptance of creation requires an important element of faith. Yes, it is true, creationists do have faith, and that faith is vitally important. In Hebrews 11:6 we read: "But without faith it is impossible to please Him, for he that cometh unto God must believe that He is, and that He is a rewarder of them that diligently seek Him." This faith is an intelligent faith, supported both by Biblical revelation and the revelation found in nature. While the *theories* and *opinions* of some scientists may contradict the Bible, there is no contradiction between the *facts* of science and the Bible.

Evolution as Faith

Of course, belief in evolution also requires a vitally important element of faith. According to one of the most popular theories on the origin of the universe, all energy and matter of the universe was once contained in a plasma ball of electrons, protons, and neutrons and other subatomic particles (how it got there, no one has the faintest notion). This huge cosmic egg then exploded—and here we are today, several billion years later, human beings with a three-pound brain composed of twelve billion neurons each connected to about ten thousand other neurons in the most complicated arrangement of matter known to man. (There are thus 120 trillion connections in the human brain.)

If this is true, then what we are and how we came to be were due solely to the properties inherent in electrons, protons, and neutrons. To believe *this* obviously requires a tremendous exercise of faith. Evolution theory is indeed no less religious nor more scientific than creation.

Evolution Is a Creation Myth

By Phillip E. Johnson

Phillip E. Johnson, a professor of law, applies his forensic skills to the theory of evolution. In the following excerpt from his book *Darwin on Trial*, Johnson tackles a key component of Darwin's theory: natural selection. Johnson argues that, while selection undoubtedly weeds out the infirm, no one has shown that it can lead to new species. The reason scientists accept it, he says, is that their commitment to naturalism rules out any possibility of intelligent design. From Johnson's perspective, this blind commitment is wholly unscientific. He argues that evolution actually constitutes the basis of a religion. As such, he says, the compulsory teaching of evolution amounts to religious indoctrination. Phillip E. Johnson is Jefferson E. Peyser Professor of Law at the University of California, Berkeley, School of Law.

D o we really know for certain that there exists some natural process by which human beings and all other living beings could have evolved from microbial ancestors, and eventually from non-living matter? When the National Academy of Sciences tells us that reliance upon naturalistic explanation is the most basic characteristic of science, is it implying that scientists somehow know that a Creator played no part in the creation of the world and its forms of life? Can something be non-science but true, or does non-science mean non*sense*? Given the emphatic endorsement of naturalistic evolution by the scientific community, can outsiders even contemplate the possibility that this officially established doctrine might be false? Well, come along and let us see.

The story of Charles Darwin has been told many times, and no wonder. The relationship with the lawyer-geologist Charles Lyell, the long voyage in the *Beagle* with the temperamental Captain Fitzroy, the observations and adventures in South America and the Galapagos Islands, the long years of preparation and delay, the eventual rushed publication of *The Origin of Species* when Alfred Russel Wallace appeared about to publish a similar theory, the controversies and the smashing triumph—all these make a great saga which is always worth another retelling. My subject is not history but the logic of current controversy, however, and so my interest must be in Darwinism and not Darwin. I am also uninterested in the differences between the theory as Darwin originally proposed it and as it is understood by neo-Darwinists today, who have the advantage of the greater understanding of genetics that science has achieved since Darwin's time. My purpose is to explain what concepts the contemporary theory employs, what significant statements about the natural world it makes, and what points of legitimate controversy there may be.

Darwin's Claims

Darwin's classic book argued three important related propositions. The first was that "the species are not immutable." By this he meant that new species have appeared during the long course of the earth's history by a natural process he called "descent with modification." The second proposition was that this evolutionary process can be extended to account for all or nearly all the diversity of life, because all living things descended from a very small number of common ancestors, perhaps a single microscopic ancestor. The third proposition, and the one most distinctive to Darwinism, was that this vast process was guided by natural selection or "survival of the fittest," a guiding force so effective that it could accomplish prodigies of biological craftsmanship that people in previous times had thought to require the guiding hand of a creator. The evidence for this third proposition is the subject of this [viewpoint].

Limits of Selection

The question is *not* whether natural selection occurs. Of course it does, and it has an effect in maintaining the genetic fitness of a population. Infants with severe birth defects do not survive to maturity without expensive medical care, and creatures which do not survive to reproduce do not leave descendants. These effects are unquestioned, but Darwinism asserts a great deal more than merely that species avoid genetic deterioration due to natural attrition among the genetically unfit. Darwinists claim that this same force of attrition has a building effect so powerful that it can begin with a bacterial cell and gradually craft its descendants over billions of years to produce such wonders as trees, flowers, ants, birds, and humans. How do we know that all this is possible?

Darwinian evolution postulates two elements. The first is what Darwin called "variation," and what scientists today call *mutation*. . . .

No Proof of Speciation

None of the "proofs" provides any persuasive reason for believing that natural selection can produce new species, new organs, or other major changes, or even minor changes that are permanent. The sickle-cell anemia case, for example, merely shows that in special circumstances an apparently disadvantageous trait may not be eliminated from the population. That larger birds have an advantage over smaller birds in high winds or droughts has no tendency whatever to prove that similar factors caused birds to come into existence in the first place. Very likely smaller birds have the advantage in other circumstances, which explains why birds are not continually becoming larger.

[French zoologist] Pierre Grassé was as unimpressed by this kind of evidence as I am, and he summarized his conclusions at the end of his chapter on evolution and natural selection:

> The "evolution in action" of [biologist] J. Huxley and other biologists is simply the observation of demographic facts, local fluctuations of genotypes, geographical distributions. Often the species concerned have remained practically unchanged for hundreds of centuries! Fluctuation as a result of circumstances, with prior modification of the genome, does not imply evolution, and we have tangible proof of this in many panchronic species [i.e., living fossils that remain unchanged for millions of years]. . . .

This conclusion seems so obviously correct that it gives rise to another problem. Why do other people, including experts whose intelligence and intellectual integrity I respect, think that evidence of local population fluctuations confirms the hypothesis that natural selection has the capacity to work engineering marvels, to construct wonders like the eye and the wing? Everyone who studies evolution knows that [H.B.D.] Kettlewell's peppered moth experiment is the classic demonstration of the power of natural selection, and that Darwinists had to wait almost a century to see even this modest confirmation of their central doctrine. Everyone who studies the experiment also knows that it has nothing to do with the origin of any species, or even any variety, because dark and white moths were present throughout the experiment. Only the ratios of one variety to the other changed. How could intelligent people have been so gullible as to imagine that the Kettlewell experiment in any way supported the ambitious claims of Darwinism? To answer that question we need to consider a fourth way in which natural selection can be formulated.

Naturalism in Science

The National Academy of Sciences told the Supreme Court that the most basic characteristic of science is "reliance upon naturalistic explanations," as opposed to "supernatural means inaccessible to human understanding." In the latter, unacceptable category contemporary scientists place not only God, but also any nonmaterial vital force that supposedly drives evolution in the direction of greater complexity, consciousness, or whatever. If science is to have any explanation for biological complexity at all it has to make do with what is left when the unacceptable has been excluded. Natural selection is the best of the remaining alternatives, probably the only alternative.

In this situation some may decide that Darwinism simply *must* be true, and for such persons the purpose of any further investigation will be merely to explain how natural selection works and to solve the mysteries created by apparent anomalies. For them there is no need to test the theory itself, for there is no respectable alternative to test it against. . . .

Evolution as God's Plan

Theistic evolution is not easy to define, but it involves making an effort to maintain that the natural world is God-governed while avoiding disagreement with the Darwinist establishment on scientific matters. Because the Darwinists have become increasingly explicit about the religious and philosophical implications of their system, this strategy led the theism in the ASA's [American Scientific Affiliation's] evolution to come under ever greater pressure.

Compatibilism has its limits, however, and some ASA leaders were prodded into action by the strong naturalistic bias of the National Academy's 1984 pamphlet, which tried to give the public the impression that science has all the major problems of evolution well in hand. With foundation support, the ASA produced its own 48-page illustrated booklet, titled *Teaching Science in a Climate of Controversy: A View from the American Scientific Affiliation*, and mailed it to thousands of schoolteachers. The general tenor of the booklet was to encourage open-mindedness, especially on such "open questions" as whether life really arose by chance, how the first animals could have evolved in the Cambrian explosion, and how human intelligence and upright posture evolved.

The ASA members who wrote *Teaching Science* naively expected that most scientists would welcome their contribution as a corrective to the overconfidence that evolutionary science tends to project when it is trying to persuade the public not to entertain any doubts. The official scientific organizations, however, are at war with creationism, and their policy is to demand unconditional surrender. Persons who claim to be scientists, but who try to convince schoolteachers that there are "open questions" about the naturalistic understanding of the world, are traitors in that war.

Retribution quickly followed. A California "science consultant" named William Bennetta, who makes a career of pursuing creationists, organized a posse of scientific heavyweights to condemn the ASA's pamphlet as "an attempt to replace science with a system of pseudoscience devoted to confirming Biblical narratives." A journal called *The Science Teacher* published a collection of essays edited by Bennetta, titled "Scientists Decry a Slick New Packaging of Creationism." Nine prominent scientists . . . contributed heavy-handed condemnations of *Teaching Science*. The pervasive message was that the ASA is a deceitful creationist front which disguises its Biblical literalist agenda under a pretence of scientific objectivity.

The accusations bewildered the authors of *Teaching Science*, and were so far off the mark that persons familiar with the ASA might easily have mistaken them for intentional misrepresentations. It would be a mistake to infer any intent to deceive, however, because really zealous scientific naturalists do not recognize subtle distinctions among theists. To the zealots, people who say they believe in God are either harmless sentimentalists who add some vague God-talk to a basically naturalistic worldview, or they are creationists. In either case they are fools, but in the latter case they are also a menace.

From a zealot's viewpoint, the ASA writers had provided ample evidence of a creationist purpose. Why would they harp on "open questions" except to imply that God might have taken a hand in the appearance of new forms? That suggestion is creationism by definition, and the ASA admits to being an organization of Christians who accept the authority of the Bible. Their true reason for rejecting scientific evolution must therefore be that it contradicts the Biblical narrative. What other reason could they have?

"Religious Humanism"

Mixing religion with science is obnoxious to Darwinists only when it is the wrong religion that is being mixed. To prove the point, we may cite two of the most important founders of the modern synthesis, Theodosius Dobzhansky and Julian Huxley. Julian Huxley's religion of "evolutionary humanism" offered humanity the "sacred duty" and the "glorious opportunity" of seeking "to promote the maximum fulfillment of the evolutionary process on the earth." That did not mean merely working to ensure that the organisms that have the most offspring continue to have the most offspring, but rather promoting the "fullest realization" of mankind's "inherent possibilities." Inspired by the same vision, the American philosopher and educational reformer John Dewey launched a movement in 1933 for "religious humanism," whose Manifesto reflected the assumption current among scientific naturalists at the time that the final demise of theistic religion would usher in a new era of scientific progress and social cooperation for mankind. Soon thereafter, Hitler and Stalin provided a stunning realization of some of mankind's inherent possibilities. Dewey's successors admitted in 1973 that a new Manifesto was needed because the events of the previous forty years had made the original statement "seem far too optimistic."

The revised Manifesto makes some unenthusiastic concessions to reality, such as that "Science has sometimes brought evil instead of good," and "Traditional religions are surely not the only obstacle to human progress." The overall message is as before. It is that salvation comes through science:

Using technology wisely, we can control our environment, conquer poverty, markedly reduce disease, extend our life-span, significantly modify our behavior, alter the course of human evolution and cultural development, unlock vast new powers, and provide humankind with unparalleled opportunity for achieving an abundant and meaningful life.

Jesuitical Embrace of Evolution

The scientist-philosopher who went farther than anybody else in drawing a message of cosmic optimism from evolution was Pierre Teilhard de Chardin, the unorthodox Jesuit paleontologist who played an important role in the Piltdown and Peking Man discoveries. Teilhard aimed to bring Christianity up to date by founding it squarely upon the rock of evolution rather that upon certain events alleged to have occurred in Palestine nearly two thousand years ago. The more rigorously materialistic Darwinists dismissed Teilhard's philosophy as pretentious claptrap, but it had a strong appeal to those of a more spiritual cast of mind, such as [biologist] Theodosius Dobzhansky.

In his reply to [social critic] Irving Kristol, [paleontologist Stephen Jay] Gould cited Dobzhansky, "the greatest evolutionist of our century and a lifelong Russian Orthodox," to illustrate the compatibility of evolution and religion. For Dobzhansky the two were a good deal more than compatible, for he wrote in his book *Mankind Evolving* that Darwin had healed "the wound inflicted by Copernicus and Galileo." This wound was the discovery that the earth, and therefore man, is not the physical center of the universe. Darwinism had healed it by placing mankind at the *spiritual* center of the universe, because man now understands evolution and has the potential capacity to take control of it. Dobzhansky exulted that "Evolution need no longer be a destiny imposed from without; it may conceivably be controlled by man, in accordance with his wisdom and his values." For further detail he referred his readers to the following quotations, which encapsulate Teilhard's "inspiring vision":

Is evolution a theory, a system, or a hypothesis? It is much more— it is a general postulate to which all theories, all hypotheses, all systems, must henceforth bow and which they must satisfy in order to be thinkable and true. Evolution is a light which illuminates all facts, a trajectory which all lines of thought must follow—this is what evolution is.

Evolution is, in short, the God we must worship. It is taking us to heaven, "The Point Omega" in Teilhard's jargon, which is:

a harmonized collectivity of consciousness, equivalent to a kind of superconsciousness. The earth is covering itself not only by myriads of thinking units, but by a single continuum of thought, and finally forming a functionally single Unit of Thought of planetary dimensions. The plurality of individual thoughts combine and mutually reinforce each other in a single act of unanimous Thought. . . . In the dimension of Thought, like in the dimension of Time and Space, can the Universe reach consummation in anything but the Measureless?

Pessimistic Darwinists

The naive optimism of these attempts to fashion a scientific religion survives in the contemporary "New Age" movement, but the trend among Darwinists today is to take a more somber view of humanity's prospects. Writing in 1989, Maitland Edey and Donald Johanson speculate that Homo sapiens may be about to make itself extinct, as a result of nuclear war or ecological catastrophe. This depressing situation is the result of a runaway technology that produces enormous quantities of toxic waste, destroys the jungle and the ozone layer, and permits unrestrained population growth. We are unable to deal intelligently with these problems because "in our guts we are passionate stone age people" who are capable of creating technology but not controlling it. Edey and Johanson think that science is about to develop the technical capacity to design "better people" through genetic engineering. If humanity is to avoid extinction, it must summon the political will to take control of evolution, and make it in the future a matter of human choice rather than blind selection.

The continual efforts to base a religion or ethical system upon evolution are not an aberration, and practically all the most prominent Darwinist writers have tried their hand at it. Darwinist evolution is an imaginative story about who we are and where we came from, which is to say it is a creation myth. As such it is an obvious starting point for speculation about how we ought to live and what we ought to value. A creationist appropriately starts with God's creation and God's will for man. A scientific naturalist just as appropriately starts with evolution and with man as a product of nature.

Evolution as a Founding Myth

In its mythological dimension, Darwinism is the story of humanity's liberation from the delusion that its destiny is controlled by a power higher than itself. Lacking scientific knowledge, humans at first attribute natural events like weather and disease to supernatural beings. As they learn to predict or control natural forces they put aside the lesser spirits, but a more highly evolved religion retains the notion of a rational Creator who rules the universe.

At last the greatest scientific discovery of all is made, and modern humans learn that they are the products of a blind natural process that has no goal and cares nothing for them. The resulting "death of God" is experienced by some as a profound loss, and by others as a liberation. But liberation to what? If blind nature has somehow produced a human species with the capacity to rule earth wisely, and if this capacity has previously been invisible only because it was smothered by superstition, then the prospects for human freedom and happiness are unbounded. That was the message of the Humanist Manifesto of 1933.

Another possibility is that purposeless nature has produced a world ruled by irrational forces, where might makes right and human freedom is an illusion. In that case the right to rule belongs to whoever can control the use of science. It would be illogical for the rulers to worry overmuch about what people say they *want*, because science teaches them that wants are the product of irrational forces. In principle, people can be made to want something better. It is no kindness to leave them as they are, because passionate stone age people can do nothing but destroy themselves when they have the power of scientific technology at their command.

Whether a Darwinist takes the optimistic or the pessimistic view, it is imperative that the public be taught to understand the world as scientific naturalists understand it. Citizens must learn to look to science as the only reliable source of knowledge, and the only power capable of bettering (or even preserving) the human condition. That implies . . . a program of indoctrination in the name of public education.

The Theory of Evolution Is Scientific

By Robert T. Pennock

According to philosopher of science Robert T. Pennock in the following selection, the arguments that creationists marshal to try to deny that evolution is scientific are flawed. For example, antievolutionists argue that if evolution occurs, the fossil record should show an uninterrupted progression of simple life-forms gradually changing to intermediate organisms, which eventually evolve into more complex ones. However, Pennock says that gaps in the record are no surprise. In the first place, the conditions that make bodies into fossils are rare, and many creatures in the past simply had no hard parts to fossilize. He also dismisses the creationist argument that observed "microevolution" within species does not provide evidence of "macroevolution" into novel species. On the contrary, Pennock argues, the burden of proof is on critics to show why a long series of tiny changes would halt at some imagined "species barrier." Fundamentally, he says, creationists err in claiming that evolution is "only" a theory and not a fact. As a scientific theory, evolution is a comprehensive explanation laden with observed facts. Robert T. Pennock earned a joint degree in biology and philosophy as an undergraduate and went on to earn a doctorate in philosophy. He teaches philosophy of science at the University of Texas–Austin.

ICR's [Institute for Creation Research's] Duane Gish argues that the fossils say "No!" to evolution, and his argument basically comes down to pointing out gaps in the fossil record.

But the so-called problem of the missing links is no news to evolutionists, and it poses no greater a threat in biology than in linguistics. After all, absence of evidence is not necessarily evidence of absence, especially when it comes to the fossil record. Paleontologists always have to contend with the possibility of preservational artifacts—absences of fossils that are due not to absences of organisms but absence of the conditions necessary for fossilization. Look around today and you can see for yourself that most of the organisms you come across are not making it into the fossil record. It takes rather special combinations of physical factors—usually those of swamps or estuaries where remains can be buried in sediment, be compacted and, if lucky, remain undisturbed for millions of years—for the bones or imprints of an organism to achieve a measure of immortality in stone. To then become part of the scientific body of evidence, they have to erode in such a way as not to be destroyed, and then found by someone who recognizes their importance. Furthermore, from what we know of evolutionary mechanisms, speciation events are likely to occur in isolated populations, and competition will quickly eliminate the less fit of closely similar forms. Both processes make it even more unlikely that there will be a smooth, continuous fossil record of intermediates. Thus, it is not at all surprising that there are "missing links" in the fossil record and this is not good evidence against evolutionary transmutation; on the contrary, given what we know, it is what we expect to see. Given the difficulties involved in fossilization in the first place the record of intermediate forms is remarkably good and continually getting better. One of the most striking new fossil discoveries involves the transition to the aquatic whale from a land mammal; surely a whale with feet counts as a transitional form. Hardly a month goes by without a major announcement of new fossil evidence that reveals more and more about the branchings of the tree of life. Even more exciting is the whole new category of fossil information that advances in genetic technology are just beginning to open up.

Fossil Gaps Are Exaggerated

Faced with the slow but steady uncovering of such new fossil evidence, [law professor Phillip E.] Johnson and other new creationists typically move quickly to what has been long considered to be the most spectacularly large gap in the fossil record, what has been called the "Cambrian explosion." Darwin himself knew of the apparently sudden appearance of animal fossils at the beginning of the Cambrian period and pointed out in *The Origin of Species* that this was problematic for his thesis of gradual evolution. At the time, however, the best he could do was hypothesize that such fossils would eventually be found. Given that the investigation of fossils was just getting off the ground in his day, this suggestion was not unreasonable. Today we have substantially more fossil information and our picture of the pathways of descent is slowly becoming clearer, but it is true that fossil evidence remains scarce for the transition into the Cambrian period, and evolutionary biology can still say rather little about those early evolutionary trails. But how big of a problem is this? Was there really not enough time, as creationists suggest, for evolution of animal phyla to occur? The Cambrian may reckon as a sudden explosion from the point of view of geologic time, but we are still talking about millions of years and this could have been quite sufficient for evolution. Much of the talk about a sudden "explosion" during the Cambrian period might be exaggerated, for example, given that recently several independent lines of new evidence suggest that animal phyla began to diverge well before the Cambrian period, during the mid-Proterozoic period about a billion years ago. Moreover, Pre-Cambrian organisms were relatively small and lacked hard parts, so their fossil record is even more sparse than usual. Certainly, the Cambrian explosion is a problem, but it is far too soon for us to pronounce it unsolvable.

Division in Creationist Ranks

Creationists' arguments about missing links in the fossil record and their claim that species are divided by unbridgeable gaps reflect a particularly unfocused form of species essentialism, the view that each species is set apart from every other by an immutable "essence." As they see it, God forms animals "according to their kinds" (Genesis 1:25–26) and they believe this implies fixity of species. It is fine, most now say, to allow limited evolution to occur within a species. However, they insist that microevolutionary changes are "strictly limited within species" and cannot extend beyond to account for macroevolutionary change from one species to another.

Some creationists today will even say that this explicit acceptance of small evolutionary changes is not a modification of their view at all, given that they have always held that the different human "nations" or "races" that went their separate ways at Babel were all evolutionarily diversified descendants of Noah's family and, originally, of Adam and Eve. However, they forget their own history and the split between the members of the antievolution Religion and Science Association (RSA), founded in 1935 by [George M.] Price and Dudley Joseph Whitney, over the possibility of limited speciation within created types. Whitney, [Frank L.] Marsh, and other more liberal members came to accept this possibility, which Price and others opposed. It should come as no surprise that the rhetoric of that debate is familiar; compromising by allowing speciation with types, said RSA conservative Byron C. Nelson would "[open] the door of evolution so wide that I, for one, don't see a place to shut it." Of course, Nelson was right, for recognizing the efficacy of evolutionary mechanisms for evolutionary change within a type is tantamount to accepting it generally.

No Clear Dividing Lines

There is no essential difference in kind between microevolution and macroevolution; the difference is simply a matter of degree. The glossary of a typical evolutionary textbook will define each as "vague" terms referring, respectively, to "small" evolutionary changes within species, or to evolutionary changes "great enough" to classify species within different genera or higher taxa. How much of a difference is "enough" varies widely from case to case. Darwin demolished the old Aristotelian notion that species are immutable in the same way that Galileo had destroyed the Aristotelian conception of the two-sphere universe. According to Aristotelian cosmology, which the Church adopted and modified to fit with its theology, the earth was at the center of the universe, and there was an essential difference in kind between its perishable terrestrial realm below the sphere of the moon and the eternal celestial realm above. Change and disintegration occurred in the sublunary region (the "microcosm"), but this had nothing to do with events in the superlunary region (the "macrocosm"). Although it was Copernicus who first seriously challenged the earth-centered view and Kepler who worked out the planetary laws for a sun-centered view, it was really Galileo who brought down the old system by providing new observations and new physical mechanisms that undermined the terrestrial and celestial essentialism. His telescopic observations that discovered the moons of Jupiter and their motions showed "terrestrial" patterns in the celestial region, and his new physics showed that supposedly distinctive "celestial" patterns of motion could be explained in terms of the same forces and laws that determined terrestrial motions. Similarly, Aristotle had held that all species were characterized by some defining essential characteristic that differentiated them from other species, and Darwin's discoveries overturned this view forever. How ironic that long after Christians come to terms with Galileo's science, which broke up the cosmological essentialism that they had taken to be a necessary part of their theology, some are still tripping over the same issue of essentialism, this time in the linguistic and biological realms.

Discoveries Yet to Come

Of course, to say that there is no essential difference between micro- and macroevolution is not to say that there are not interesting and perhaps significant differences at some higher taxonomic levels. For example, spurred in part by the punctuated equilibria model of evolutionary change, proposed by Stephen Jay Gould and Niles Eldredge, many biologists expect that there are still discoveries to be made of biological constraints that might have been relevant in the development and stability of the approximately thirty-five body plans of the major phyla. The developmental biologist Rudolf Raff has written about some of the research that is beginning to bloom in this area. It is likely that additional causal factors will be confirmed as research in developmental biology broadens the modern evolutionary synthesis. However, this will do nothing to change the basic facts of evolution that are already well confirmed. Nor will it negate the reasonable inference from small changes observed in what is taken at one time to be one species, to accumulations and divergences of these changes to such a degree that we should classify later populations as distinct species. It simply will not do for creationists to admit that microevolution is true within species and then turn around and claim that this has nothing to do with the macroevolution of one species into others. If creationists think each species has some essentially distinctive, immutable features that prevent speciation then let us hear what they are. Of course, they have nothing of the kind to offer.

Incredibly, Phillip Johnson thinks that he has dismissed the inference from observed small-scale changes to large ones with a single argument. He says that Darwinists need to supply "a scientific theory of how macroevolution can occur," and that for them to infer that "small changes add up to big ones" by reference to a principle of uniformity is simply to appeal to "an arbitrary philosophical principle." But there is nothing arbitrary about a principle that regards observed causal mechanisms as operating uniformly, and, unlike creationism, evolutionary theory has identified a clear set of relevant mechanisms. Consider the chromosomes and sequences of DNA not only within species but across genera, phyla, and other higher order taxa. Whether we are looking at ducks or daisies, nematodes or human beings, we find the same genetic material, the same or similar genes, and so on. Start with the genome of one species and with only a fraction of a percent change—some additions, deletions and rearrangements of those Ts, As, Gs, and Cs—you have the genome of a different species. Furthermore, the processes that transform and select these sequences are common across the board. Thus the theory, the observational evidence, and the uniformity principle work hand in hand here, as they always do in science. The burden of proof is on the critic to show that there is some barrier—a difference in essential kind rather than degree.

Numerical Standards Lacking

There is no fixed number of differences in the sequences that distinguishes change within a species from change across species, and it is hard to imagine how one could even attempt to draw such a line. Do creationists define acceptable "microevolution" as anything below a hundred changes? A million? Pick any number; somewhere along the way there will be a sufficient difference to distinguish species; why would creationists think then that it is reasonable to have just so many changes but no more? A hundred but not a hundred and one? A million but not a million one hundred? How can they accept that small changes accumulate up to that number, and then turn around and say that scientists are appealing to an arbitrary principle when they infer that those same small changes just added up a bit more?

It is a pity that Johnson fails to practice what he preaches. In demanding that Darwinists supply a theory of how macroevolution can occur (and blithely dismissing the well confirmed theory they have), he himself is completely silent about how it is supposed to happen according to his own creationist alternative. Indeed, though "intelligent design" is proffered as the "better theory," Johnson and other IDC [intelligent design creationism] "theorists" consistently refuse to reveal anything positive about their theory. It is easy to point out missing links in any scientific theory for science lays its commitments and its evidence on the table and identifies in every research report the gaps still to be filled. On the other hand, it is impossible to find empirical holes in Johnson's creationism, for his notion makes no empirical contact with the world at all; the "theory" of intelligent design begins and ends with God's creative power. It is not just links that are missing here; what is missing is any semblance of a theory at all. . . .

New Puzzles

Of course, we are in no position to bridge every chasm; there remain any number of gaps that have yet to be explained, allowing creationists to bring up different puzzles each year and quietly drop old ones that have been solved. However, the history of evolutionary biology is a history of apparent explanatory gaps that scientists have closed one by one. Recall how the discovery of Mendelian genetics provided the solution to the problem of blending inheritance. When I was an undergraduate biology major, my professors noted that no one could explain the mechanism by which the spindle fibers formed and segregated chromosomes during cell division; fifteen years later the newly discovered answer would fill in that gap in the textbooks. It would be easy to multiply such examples, for evolution has been and remains a progressive, successful research program.

When we consider [biochemist Michael] Behe's criticisms in light of this consistent pattern, his book becomes particularly significant in that it indicates just how far creationists have had to retreat to find significant explanatory gaps in evolutionary theory. Behe is certainly correct that molecular biology has identified a host of new and heretofore unappreciated puzzles for evolutionary biologists. That they have yet to solve, or in many cases even to begin to address these puzzles, however, is mostly the unsurprising result of the fact that molecular biology is still a very new subdiscipline. Many of the most significant molecular techniques that are now allowing biologists to look inside the black box of the cell were developed just in the last decade or two. The opening of this final box has indeed revealed a new level of complexity that has yet to be explained. But what should we conclude from our ignorance about such matters? Should we applaud and encourage the new generation of graduate students in molecular biology who are now eagerly turning their attention to investigating, and perhaps discovering the solutions of these puzzles? Or should we, as Behe and other creationists suggest, judge that these explanatory gaps are uncrossable by evolutionary or any natural theory and conclude that intervention by a divine intelligent designer is the only possible explanation? . . .

I hope the conclusion to draw is obvious. All the creationists' challenges that "Science cannot explain X" are nothing but what philosophers call "arguments from ignorance." To point out that we are ignorant of the scientific explanation of X is hardly good reason to conclude that God is the explanation. To call upon God to plug our explanatory gaps in such cases is tantamount to intellectual indolence. No doubt God could plug these or any purported gap, but surely God has better things to do. . . .

"Just a Theory"

When creationists press their agenda at school board meetings and on the editorial pages of newspapers they often argue that evolution is "just a theory." They try to introduce legislation and lobby for changes of wording in science curricula to emphasize this view. One notorious example occurred in 1996 in Tennessee. Creationists had successfully put such language into Senate Bill 3229 (sec. 49-6-1012), a proposed law that said:

> No teacher or administrator in a local education agency shall teach the theory of evolution except as a scientific theory.

Biology teachers reading through to just this line found it a bit funny and rather perplexing, since of course evolution is a scientific theory and it would seem bizarre to legislate this. They did not laugh at the punch line that followed, however, which said:

> Any teacher or administrator teaching such theory as fact commits insubordination . . . and shall be dismissed or suspended.

It was as though Tennessee creationists were bucking for a replay of the Monkey Trial seventy-one years later, and this time Scopes would not get away with just a guilty verdict and a fine. Fortunately, reason prevailed in this instance and the measure was defeated 20 to 13 after a five-hour floor debate, saving Tennessee from the embarrassment of being seen as a laughingstock. But as we have already noted, other states have passed less draconian but equally absurd laws mandating that in classrooms evolution should be taught "as theory, not fact."

Fancy Word for "Guess"

The contrast that creationists want to draw is clear. When they say that evolution is only a theory they put the emphasis on "only." In the logically slippery way they portray the situation, facts are true, theories are not facts, evolution is a theory, and thus evolution is not a fact and so is not true. These claims have been repeated often enough by creationist activists that it is now one of the most common arguments that one hears from people when they oppose evolution in a public forum.

> Evolution is only a theory. It should not be taught as fact in our public schools. If the evolutionist theory is taught, then it is only fair that Creationism be presented. It takes more faith to believe in evolution than it does to believe in divine creation.

They also draw the conclusion that creationists want:

> Creation and Evolution are just theories. "Theory" is just a fancy word for "guess."

Along the same lines is the claim that evolution is just an "assumption." We find this kind of charge reiterated throughout creationist literature. In *A Case for Creation*, Wayne Frair and Percival Davis write,

> Every age has possessed certain unquestioned presuppositions that served as foundations for its most popular philosophies. Such a presupposition in our day is the theory of evolution.

My guide at ICR's Museum of Creation took pains to emphasize this point as well. Phillip Johnson sometimes makes the same charge that evolution is an assumption, although elsewhere he is more subtle, arguing that it is scientific naturalism that is an "arbitrary assumption" and that evolutionary theory depends upon it. . . .

It is certainly true that evolutionary theory is a scientific theory, but it is equally certain that it is not a "guess." So what are we to make of the creationists' challenge?

The Meaning of Scientific Theory

In part, this is simply a problem of terminology; as we saw before, the way terms are used in everyday contexts often are significantly different from how they are used in the context of a technical discipline. What in ordinary speech we might call "just a theory" corresponds more closely to what scientists would call an "untested hypothesis." When a scientist puts forward a new hypothesis about how the world is (or, put another way, proposes a model of some aspect of the world) it is typically an *educated* guess, but it does not have to be even that and may have been thought of at random or in a dream. The real scientific work consists in taking this hypothesis and checking to see whether it can survive the rigors of logical and empirical testing. Hypotheses are tested within an explanatory framework and if they are confirmed they may be added to that framework. The whole structure of hypotheses and models and their explanatory interrelationships constitutes a theory.

Look back now at the theory of language evolution and you will see the outline of such a structure. [Sir William] Jones's common source hypothesis was originally proposed and tested in the context of a relatively small number of languages that were recognized as Indo-European but then became part of a general theoretical framework that included the notion of language families, mechanisms of linguistic variation, transmission and transformation, rules for identification of homologous structures that indicate pathways of descent, and so on. All these explanatory elements and more are what make sense of the changes of spelling, symbols, words, and grammar, the patterns of spatial and temporal distribution of languages, and the myriad other patterns of commonalities and differences linguists find among languages. This whole interconnected structure of confirmed hypotheses is the theory of the evolution of languages. The theory of evolution of biological organisms, as we have seen, has a similar complex structure. To confuse this scientific, technical notion of theory with the colloquial notion of a theory as just a guess or an assumption is simply a mistake that arises out of ignorance of science.

Laden with Facts

Once we are clear about what a theory is as the term is used in science, we should recognize that it does not stand in contrast to the notion of a fact. Quite the contrary. Jones's original hypothesis of common descent is not "*just* a theory." It is not an "assumption." It is not a "guess." Languages do descend one from another. That is a fact. And that fact is part of a strong fabric of interwoven facts that are all part of the theory of the evolution of languages. Theories may include statements of direct observations, models of mechanisms and processes, conclusions about unobservables expressed in a technical vocabulary, and so on, and all these may properly be considered factual. At this point, the theory of the evolution of languages has such overwhelming evidence supporting it that one finds it hard to conceive how it could possibly be overturned, though of course it might be refined, modified, or extended. The same can be said of other scientific theories such as that of the cellular organization of living organisms (cell theory), that dealing with the attraction of masses to one another (theory of gravitation), and so on. Atomic theory, the special and general theories of relativity, quantum theory, and, yes, the theory of biological evolution are all similarly well established.

Creationist Arguments Against Evolution Are Faulty

By Niles Eldredge

In this selection paleontologist Niles Eldredge takes on the claims of creationists. He rebuts their argument that the fossil record does not support evolution because it contains "gaps" where intermediates between ancient and contemporary creatures should appear. Fossilization and fossil survival are rare events, so gaps, he says, are to be expected. Although the fossil record is much more revealing than creationists are willing to admit, he says, evolutionary theory predicts that intermediates will be especially rare. This rarity is caused by the fact that species divide when two different survival strategies pay off. If, for example, being either swift and light or strong and slow promotes survival, those individuals who are in the middle tend to die off fast. Eldredge faults the creationists' refusal to accept archaeopteryx as an intermediate between reptilians and birds, when clearly this ancient winged creature is just such an intermediate. However, Eldredge is most critical of the creationist attitude toward the fossil record of human ancestors. The opponents of evolution, he says, simply refuse to accept the mounting evidence of hominid ancestors. Niles Eldredge, a longtime collaborator with the late Stephen Jay Gould, is a curator at the American Museum of Natural History in New York.

Niles Eldredge, *The Triumph of Evolution and the Failure of Creationism*. New York: A Peter N. Nevraumont Book, Nevraumont Publishing Company, Inc., 2000. Copyright © 2000 by Niles Eldredge. Reproduced by permission of Henry Holt and Company, LLC.

C reationists say there can be variation within kinds (microevolution) but not between kinds (macroevolution—"real evolution" to [creationist author] Gary Parker). Biologists assert that there has been one history of life: all life has descended from a single common ancestor; therefore one process—evolution—is responsible for the diversity we see. Creationists insist on two separate theories: (1) the creation of these nebulous basic kinds by a supernatural Creator, followed by (2) microevolution producing variation within those basic kinds. They admit they have no scientific evidence for the first phase.

There is a commonly followed maxim in science (often called Occam's razor) that the simpler idea in general is to be favored over a more complex one when there is no compelling reason to proceed otherwise. The dualistic structure of the creation-science model is a vastly more complicated notion (however barren this structure might be of actual concrete ideas, not to mention evidence) than the simple notion that all life has descended from a single common ancestor—no matter how rich and complex may be the ideas about how that process has worked to produce life's history and present-day diversity.

Dealing with Fossil Gaps

Creationists love gaps, lack of any obviously intermediate forms between dogs and cats, insectivores and bats, lizards and birds, fishes and frogs, and so on, and better yet the supposed absence of intermediates in the fossil record. Gaps, to creationists, are the Achilles' heel, the fatal flaw, of biological evolution.

Evolutionary biologists remain unperturbed by the gap problem for several very good reasons: (1) The evidence of connectedness and continuity—whether on a small scale between closely related (often nearly indistinguishable) species, or on larger scales—is simply much better than the creationists claim. In addition, (2) . . . beginning with [geneticist Theodosius] Dobzhansky's work in the 1930s, evolutionary biologists have come to realize that *the evolutionary process itself—especially via speciation—automatically creates a measure of discontinuity.* And, as Darwin himself noted, (3) many species that would appear as intermediates are now extinct: for example, the australopithecine species, as well as *Homo habilis, Homo ergaster*, and *Homo erectus* are now all extinct, so anyone who would claim close evolutionary connections between chimps and humans (based for example, on their remarkably high percentage of shared genes) nonetheless does not have the benefit of lots of intermediate species, since those intermediates are now extinct. Fortunately, we do have them in the fossil record! Finally, as Darwin also pointed out, (4) we cannot possibly expect to find the remains of all species that have ever lived, for several reasons: the sedimentary record itself is too discontinuous ("gappy"), much has been destroyed by erosion already, fossils tend to be destroyed by chemicals in the groundwaters percolating through rocks (not to mention the ravages of metamorphism), most sediments remain deeply buried and thus inaccessible, and for the most part only animals and plants with tough tissues (e.g., shells, bones, wood) are likely to be fossilized in the first place. With all those things to go against it, the fossil record emerges as a true marvel, and it has produced many series of intermediates. . . . Let's consider one additional, classic example—one that shows up time and time again in zoology texts and creationist tracts alike: the Mesozoic reptile-bird known as *Archaeopteryx.*

Disputes over Archaeopteryx

The case of *Archaeopteryx* makes it clear that one person's intermediate is another's basic kind, or failing that, outright fraud. Paleontologists point to examples from their own work, and creationists respond by refusing to accept the examples as intermediates. To evolutionary biologists, *Archaeopteryx* is beautifully intermediate between advanced archosaurian reptiles and birds. In contrast, creationists don't say that *Archaeopteryx* is a fake; to them, it's just another bird. It isn't.

Archaeopteryx comes from Upper Jurassic limestones of Bavaria. The seven known specimens are about 150 million years old. Zoologists have known for years that birds are effectively feathered reptiles (dinosaurs, actually), because there are so relatively few anatomical differences between birds and living reptiles, and even fewer between birds and the archosaurian reptiles (including dinosaurs) of Mesozoic times. Birds have some evolutionary specializations not found in reptiles: in addition to their uniquely constructed wings, they lack teeth and have feathers, four-chambered hearts, and horny bills.

[Creation biologist Duane] Gish says of *Archaeopteryx,* "The so-called intermediate is no real intermediate at all because, as paleontologists acknowledge, *Archaeopteryx* was a true bird—it had wings, it was completely feathered, it flew. . . . It was not a half-way bird, it was a bird". In other words, since evolutionists classify *Archaeopteryx* as a bird, then a bird it is, not some kind of intermediate between reptiles and birds. Semantic games aside, it is certainly accurate to see birds as little more than feathered archosaurs. Feathers, wings, and a bill are three evolutionary novelties that *Archaeopteryx* shares with all later birds, and these new features are the ones that allow us to recognize the evolutionary group birds. But all living birds lack teeth and bony tails, and they have well-developed keeled breastbones to support strong flight muscles. *Archaeopteryx* lacks such a keel but still retains the teeth and bony tail typical of its reptilian ancestors.

The reason why *Archaeopteryx* so delights paleontologists is that *evolutionary theory expects that new characteristics—the "evolutionary novelties" that define a group—will not appear all at the same time in the evolutionary history of the lineage.* Some new characters will appear before others. Indeed, the entire concept of an intermediate hinges on this expectation. Creationists imply that any intermediate worthy of the name must exhibit an even gradation between primitive and advanced conditions of each and every anatomical feature. But there is no logical reason to demand of evolution that it smoothly modify all parts simultaneously. It is far more reasonable to expect that at each stage some features will be relatively more advanced than others; intermediates worthy of the name would have a mosaic of primitive retentions of the ancestral condition, some in-between characters, and the fully evolved, advanced condition in yet other anatomical features. *Archaeopteryx* had feathered wings, but the keeled sternum necessary for truly vigorous flight had not yet been developed in the avian lineage. And *Archaeopteryx* still had the reptilian tail, teeth, and claws on its wings.

Twisted Logic

Creationists point to some living birds that, while still young, have poorly developed keels or claws on their wings (as is the case with the South American hoatzin). They also point to Cretaceous birds, younger than *Archaeopteryx* that still had teeth. Here is the height of twisted logic: creationists say, "Look here—there are some modern and fossil species of birds with some of the supposed intermediate or primitive reptilian features that are out of the correct position in time." Instead of interpreting these birds as primitive links to the past, creationists see them as somehow a challenge to *Archaeopteryx* as a gap-filling intermediate.

The whole point about intermediates, though, is that ancestral features are frequently retained while newer features are being added to another part of the body. It was not for another 80 million years or so that birds finally lost their teeth—though they had lost their tails in the meantime. That juvenile stages of descendants often show features of their adult ancestors, as in the hoatzin's juvenile claw, prompted the German evolutionary biologist Ernst Haeckel's famous nineteenth-century maxim "ontogeny recapitulates phylogeny," meaning that the evolutionary history of an animal is in a sense repeated in its development from egg to adult. Bluster as they might, creationists cannot wriggle away from *Archaeopteryx*.

Creationists Confront Human Evolution

The case the creationists care about most—and quite possibly the *only* case they care about—is the origin of humans, *Homo sapiens*, us. And it is indeed ironic that delineating humans as a basic created kind separated by profound and unbridgeable gaps from the living great apes and extinct species of hominids is a task of Herculean proportions, a challenge that so far has evoked only a feeble response from creationism's leading exponents. Creationists have had pitifully little to say about this, their worst nightmare: the overwhelming genetic and anatomical evidence of connections between humans and the great apes (and, through the apes, with the rest of life), and the dense and rich fossil record of human evolution.

What do the creationists say about human evolution? Creationists such as Gish and Parker agree with anthropologists that younger fossils are very modern in appearance, though they don't admit that anatomically modern human fossils from southern Africa are over a hundred thousand years old, and that modern humans arrived in Europe around thirty-five thousand years ago. They also like to revive the old canard that, with a necktie and coat on, a Neanderthal man would pass unnoticed in the New York subways. I sincerely doubt it, since most paleoanthropologists have generally concluded that Neanderthals were a distinct species.

Early Hominids

Skipping back 3 million years or so, we find various species of the genus *Australopithecus*, whose name means (as creationists fondly point out) "southern ape" and thereby, on linguistic grounds alone—automatically, in the creationist book—is a form of ape and no member of the human lineage. Assessing zoological relationships on such etymological grounds is rather dubious, to say the least, but the creationists' claim that "it looks like an ape, so call it an ape" greatly insults these remote ancestors and collateral kin of ours. They had upright posture and a bipedal gait, and some of them, at least, fashioned tools in a distinctive style. No apes these, but rather primitive hominids looking and acting just about the way you would expect them to so soon after our lineage split off from the line that became the modern great apes.

But it is the fossils of the middle 1.5 million years I just skipped over that make creationists writhe. Here we have *Homo erectus*, first known to the world as *Pithecanthropus erectus* (literally "erect ape-man"), based on specimens from Java, and as *Sinanthropus pekinensis* ("Peking man") from China. Now known from Africa as well (in the form of the closely related species, *Homo ergaster*), the *Homo erectus* lineage lived virtually unchanged for over 1.5 million years and was, by all appearances, a singularly successful species. *Homo erectus* had fire and made elaborate stone tools, and its brain size was intermediate between that of the older African fossils and the later, modern-looking specimens. Specimens of *Homo erectus* don't look like apes, yet they don't look exactly like us, either. To most of us, *Homo erectus* looks exactly like an intermediate between modern humans and our more remote ancestors.

Charges of Fakery

What do creationists do with *Homo erectus?* No problem: *Homo erectus* is a fake in the creationist lexicon. Gish asks us to recall Piltdown, that famous forgery—evidence of skulduggery in the ranks of learned academe. And what, the creationists ask, about *Hesperopithecus haroldcookii* ("Nebraska man"), described years ago on the basis of a single tooth, which later turned out to have belonged to a pig? (Scientists do make mistakes, and pig and human molars are rather similar, presumably a reflection of similar diets.) So it is, they say, with *Homo erectus*. According to Gish, the Java fossils were just skullcaps of apes wrongly associated with a modern human thighbone. And the original Peking fossils are now gone, apparently lost by a contingent of U.S. marines evacuating China in the face of the Japanese invasion of World War II. Hmmm, very suspicious, say the creationists. Never mind the casts of the originals, the drawings and photographs plus detailed written descriptions of these fossils published by the scholar Franz Weidenreich. And never mind that the Chinese have since found more skulls at the original site, or that Richard Leakey has found the closely related species, *Homo ergaster*, beautifully preserved in East Africa.

That the best the creationists can do with the human fossil record is call the most recent fossils fully human, the earliest merely apes, and those in the middle—the intermediates, if you will—outright fakes is pathetic. Humans are about the worst example of a basic kind that creationists could have chosen. The irony is great: the case toward which all their passion for producing propaganda is ultimately directed—how *we* got here—is about the most difficult one I can think of to support the model of creation.

Glen Rose Footprints

It would certainly be helpful to the creationist cause if all organisms could be shown to have appeared at the same time in the rock record—the result of one grand creative act by God—or, failing that, at least a grand commingling of extinct and modern forms of life all deposited together by Noah's Flood. Thus creationists have taken great delight in the supposedly human footprints alongside bona fide dinosaur tracks in the Cretaceous Glen Rose Formation, exposed in the channel of the Paluxy River in Texas. Here, they proclaim, is direct evidence that humans and dinosaurs roamed the Earth together, just as it was written in *Alley Oop*. Gary Parker is quite suave as he describes fitting his own feet into these impressions. But none other than a creationist (B. Neufeld, in his article "Dinosaur Tracks and Giant Men," 1975) has blown the whistle on these tracks. Alas for the creationist cause, they aren't footprints at all; the few "human" impressions visible these days do not show any signs of "squishing" of the sedimentary layers either at the edges or directly beneath the "tracks" (as the dinosaur prints, incidentally, clearly do). And, according to Neufeld, during the Great Depression it was a common local practice to chisel out human footprints to enhance tourist interest—a practice akin to the recent fabrication of Bigfoot footprints in the Pacific Northwest. Need anything more be said about the quality and trustworthiness of creationists' dealings with the fossil record?

CHAPTER 4

New Currents in Evolution

Sex and Evolution

By Matt Ridley

The difficult thing to understand about sex, author Matt Ridley explains in the following selection from his book *The Red Queen*, is to explain why creatures do not just clone themselves and thereby pass along 100 percent of their genes instead of just half of them through sex. The answer, Ridley says, may be that sex provides a crucial advantage to creatures that are constantly under siege from microbial parasites. With each generation, he says, parasites begin to adapt to whatever defenses their host may have developed. Sex, however, allows creatures to reshuffle their genes in each generation, keeping parasites a step behind. Since parasites are often a deadly threat, the genetic cost of sex is more than made up for by the change in genes in every generation. Matt Ridley, a former scientist, is the author of several acclaimed books on evolutionary insights into human nature.

I magine a Stone Age cave inhabited by two men and two women, one of them a virgin. One day the virgin gives birth "asexually" to a baby girl that is essentially her identical twin. (She becomes, in the jargon, a "parthenogen.") It could happen in several ways—for example, by a process called "automixis," in which an egg is, roughly speaking, fertilized by another egg. The cave woman has another daughter two years later by the same means. Her sister, meanwhile, has had a son and a daughter by the normal method. There are now eight people in the cave. Next, the three young girls each have two children and the first generation dies off. Now there are ten people in the cave, but five of them are parthenogens. In two generations the gene for parthenogenesis has spread from one-quarter to one-half of the population. It will not be long before men are extinct.

This is what [evolutionary biologist George C.] Williams called the cost of meiosis and [engineer-turned-biologist John] Maynard Smith called the cost of males. For what dooms the sexual cave

Matt Ridley, *The Red Queen: Sex and the Evolution of Human Nature*. New York: Perennial, 1993. Copyright © 1993 by Matt Ridley. Reproduced by permission of Scribner, an imprint of Simon & Schuster Adult Publishing Group.

people is simply that half of them are men, and men do not produce babies. It is true that men do occasionally help in child rear-
ing, killing woolly rhinos for dinner or whatever, but even that
does not really explain why men are necessary. . . .

This thought-experiment illustrates the numerically huge advantage a gene that makes its owner asexual has. Logic such as
this set Maynard Smith, [biologist Michael] Ghiselin, and
Williams to wondering what compensating advantage of sex there
must be, given that every mammal and bird, most invertebrate animals, most plants and fungi, and many protozoa are sexual. . . .

Ceaseless Competition

Enter, running, the Red Queen. This peculiar monarch became
part of biological theory twenty years ago [circa 1973,] and has
been growing ever more important in the years since then. Follow
me if you will into a dark labyrinth of stacked shelves in an office
at the University of Chicago, past ziggurats of balanced books and
three-foot Babels of paper. Squeeze between two filing cabinets
and emerge into a Stygian space the size of a broom cupboard,
where sits an oldish man in a checked shirt and with a gray beard
that is longer than God's but not so long as Charles Darwin's. This
is the Red Queen's first prophet, Leigh Van Valen, a single-minded
student of evolution. One day in 1973, before his beard was so
gray, Van Valen was searching his capacious mind for a phrase to
express a new discovery he had made while studying marine fossils. The discovery was that the probability a family of animals
would become extinct does not depend on how long that family
has already existed. In other words, species do not get better at
surviving (nor do they grow feeble with age, as individuals do).
Their chances of extinction are random.

The significance of this discovery had not escaped Van Valen,
for it represented a vital truth about evolution that Darwin had not
wholly appreciated. The struggle for existence never gets easier.
However well a species may adapt to its environment, it can never
relax, because its competitors and its enemies are also adapting to
their niches. Survival is a zero-sum game. Success only makes one
species a more tempting target for a rival species. Van Valen's
mind went back to his childhood and lit upon the living chess
pieces that Alice encountered beyond the looking glass [in Lewis
Carroll's novel *Beyond the Looking Glass*]. The Red Queen is a

formidable woman who runs like the wind but never seems to get anywhere:

"Well, in *our* country," said Alice, still panting a little, "you'd generally get to somewhere else—if you ran very fast for a long time as we've been doing."

"A slow sort of country!" said the Queen. "Now, *here*, you see, it takes all the running *you* can do to keep in the same place. If you want to get to somewhere else, you must run at least twice as fast as that!"

"A new evolutionary law," wrote Van Valen, who sent a manuscript to each of the most prestigious scientific journals, only to see it rejected. Yet his claim was justified. The Red Queen has become a great personage in the biological court. And nowhere has she won a greater reputation than in theories of sex.

Sex as a Defense

Red Queen theories hold that the world is competitive to the death. It does keep changing. But did we not just hear that species are static for many generations and do not change? Yes. The point about the Red Queen is that she runs but stays in the same place. The world keeps coming back to where it started; there is change but not progress.

Sex, according to the Red Queen theory, has nothing to do with adapting to the inanimate world—becoming bigger or better camouflaged or more tolerant of cold or better at flying—but is all about combating the enemy that fights back.

Biologists have persistently overestimated the importance of physical causes of premature death rather than biological ones. In virtually any account of evolution, drought, frost, wind, or starvation looms large as the enemy of life. . . .

Killer Plagues

The things that kill animals or prevent them from reproducing are only rarely physical factors. Far more often other creatures are involved—parasites, predators, and competitors. A water flea that is starving in a crowded pond is the victim not of food shortage but of competition. Predators and parasites probably cause most of the world's deaths, directly or indirectly. When a tree falls in the forest, it has usually been weakened by a fungus. When a herring meets its end, it is usually in the mouth of a bigger fish or in a net. What killed your ancestors two centuries or more ago? Smallpox, tuberculosis, influenza, pneumonia, plague, scarlet fever, diarrhea. Starvation or accidents may have weakened people, but infection killed them. A few of the wealthier ones died of old age or cancer or heart attacks, but not many.

The "great war" of 1914–18 killed 25 million people in four years. The influenza epidemic that followed killed 25 million in four months. It was merely the latest in a series of devastating plagues to hit the human species after the dawn of civilization. Europe was laid waste by measles after A.D. 165, by smallpox after A.D. 251, by bubonic plague after 1348, by syphilis after 1492, and by tuberculosis after 1800. And those are just the epidemics. Endemic diseases carried away additional vast numbers of people. Just as every plant is perpetually under attack from insects, so every animal is a seething mass of hungry bacteria waiting for an opening. There may be more bacterial than human cells in the object you proudly call "your" body. There may be more bacteria in and on you as you read this than there are human beings in the whole world.

Focus on Parasites

Again and again in recent years evolutionary biologists have found themselves returning to the theme of parasites. As Richard Dawkins put it in a recent paper: "Eavesdrop [over] morning coffee at any major centre of evolutionary theory today, and you will find 'parasite' to be one of the commonest words in the language. Parasites are touted as the prime movers in the evolution of sex, promising a final solution to that problem of problems."

Parasites have a deadlier effect than predators for two reasons. One is that there are more of them. Human beings have no predators except great white sharks and one another, but they have lots of parasites. Even rabbits, which are eaten by stoats, weasels, foxes, buzzards, dogs, and people, are host to far more fleas, lice, ticks, mosquitoes, tapeworms, and uncounted varieties of protozoa, bacteria, fungi, and viruses. The myxomatosis virus has killed far more rabbits than have foxes. The second reason, which is the cause of the first, is that parasites are usually smaller than their hosts, while predators are usually larger. This means that the parasites live shorter lives and pass through more generations in a given time than their hosts. The bacteria in your gut pass through six times as many generations during your lifetime as people have passed through since they were apes. As a consequence, they can multiply faster than their hosts and control or reduce the host population. The predator merely follows the abundance of its prey.

Parasites and their hosts are locked in a close evolutionary embrace. The more successful the parasite's attack (the more hosts it infects or the more resources it gets from each), the more the host's chances of survival will depend on whether it can invent a defense. The better the host defends, the more natural selection will promote the parasites that can overcome the defense. So the advantage will always be swinging from one to the other: The more dire the emergency for one, the better it will fight. This is truly the world of the Red Queen, where you never win, you only gain a temporary respite.

Like an Arms Race

It is also the inconstant world of sex. Parasites provide exactly the incentive to change genes every generation that sex seems to demand. The success of the genes that defended you so well in the last generation may be the best of reasons to abandon these same gene combinations in the next. By the time the next generation comes around, the parasites will have surely evolved an answer to the defense that worked best in the last generation. It is a bit like sport. In chess or in football, the tactic that proves most effective is soon the one that people learn to block easily. Every innovation in attack is soon countered by another in defense.

But of course the usual analogy is an arms race. America builds an atom bomb, so Russia does, too. America builds missiles; so must Russia. Tank after tank, helicopter after helicopter, bomber after bomber, submarine after submarine, the two countries run against each other, yet stay in the same place. Weapons that would have been invincible twenty years before are now vulnerable and obsolete. The bigger the lead of one superpower, the harder the other tries to catch up. Neither dares step off the treadmill while it can afford to stay in the race.

How Mothers Shape Evolution

By Sarah Blaffer Hrdy

In the following selection anthropologist Sarah Blaffer Hrdy argues that maternal choices have a far richer variety of effects on evolution than previously recognized. According to Hrdy, research has begun to reveal a wide range of strategies that mothers use to assure reproductive success—the only kind of success that counts in evolution. Some breed quickly and then leave their young to fend for themselves. Others invest years in raising a relatively few offspring. Some mothers will kill the weakest members of their litters to better the chances of the rest to survive. Among social species, such as chimpanzees, mothers compete for status, form alliances, and even kill the babies of rivals. Trained as an anthropologist, Sarah Blaffer Hrdy has become a notable contributor to evolutionary theory and primatology. She has taught at the University of California, Davis.

For each mother, life is a series of turning points and decisions mostly about how best to allocate resources over the course of her lifetime, be it long or short. Should she put all her effort into growing big, producing a large number of offspring all at once, breed in a single fecund burst like the salmon who forage in the ocean, swim upstream, spawn, and die? (This is known as semelparity.) Or should she bear fewer offspring, with births spaced at long intervals over a long life (iteroparity), like chimpanzees or humans do?

A survey of the natural world through the lens of this life-historical approach reveals just how special a creature the self-sacrificing mother envisioned by men like the French physician [Jean-Emanuel] Gilibert must be. Such mothers exist, but they do not evolve as species-typical universals of the female sex except

Sarah Blaffer Hrdy, *Mother Nature: Maternal Instincts and How They Shape the Human Species.* New York: Pantheon Books, 1999. Copyright © 1999 by Sarah Blaffer Hrdy. Reproduced by permission of Pantheon Books, a division of Random House, Inc.

under the most stringent circumstances. Typically, self-sacrificing mothers are found in highly inbred groups, or when mothers are nearing the end of their reproductive careers. The breed-and-then-die strategy typical of semelparous creatures (who reproduce only once in their lifetime) provides the best examples.

One-Time Breeders

If semelparity is hard to visualize, think of Charlotte, the altruistic spider mother in E.B. White's beloved children's book *Charlotte's Web*. She toils and spins to lay her single pouch of eggs, and when her life's work is done, she dies. This is classic semelparous reproduction.

A human mother who feels put-upon by the onslaught of child-related demands when she arrives home after a long day at work may be heartened to know how much better off she is than one of these more "selfless" mothers. Semelparous mothers are often literally "eaten alive" by their young.

The prize for "extreme maternal care" goes to one of the various matriphagous (yes, it means mother-eating) spiders. After laying her eggs, an Australian social spider (*Diaea ergandros*) continues to store nutrients in a new batch of eggs—odd, oversized eggs, far too large to pass through her oviducts, and lacking genetic instructions. Since she breeds only once, what are they for?

These eggs are for eating, not for laying. But to be eaten by whom? As the spiderlings mature and begin to mill about, the mother becomes strangely subdued. She starts to turn mushy— but in a liquefying rather than a sentimental way. As her tissue melts, her ravenous young literally suck her up, starting with her legs and eventually devouring the protein-rich eggs dissolving within her.

Few things seem quite so antisocial as cannibalism. Yet dining on mother may be the key ingredient to the evolution of these spiders' unusually gregarious lifestyle. By having the bad manners to eat their mother, sated spiderlings are rendered less likely to eat one another. Furthermore, even among selfless mothers, not all are equal. There is room for all sorts of selection on each mother's attributes. The more efficient a mother is at capturing prey, the bigger she gets; the bigger she is, the bigger the banquet she provides and the less inclined her progeny are to eat each other and the more her little cannibals reap the benefits of a social existence.

Mammal Mothers

Few mammals breed in one semelparous bang. Instead, most are iteroparous, breeding sequentially over a lifetime. Such mothers may produce young singly or in litters. For creatures like ourselves, shaped by this iteroparous potential to breed more than once, it rarely makes sense for a female to put all her eggs in one basket. An iteroparous mother who overshoots the optimum clutch-size for her circumstances, whose ovaries are bigger than her larder, may lose her entire brood to starvation or end up so weak she does not breed next season when conditions improve. Worse, she may succumb trying.

Learning just how mothers allocate their time and energy between making a living, resting, and reproducing, or caring for infants became the goal of primatologist Jeanne Altmann. She and her husband, Stuart, had set out in 1963 to study the ecology and social behavior of baboons on the dusty plains of Amboseli, in Kenya. Their landmark study, which continues to the present day, would also provide the first opportunity to investigate the trade-offs that primate mothers make. Her research on the ecology of mothers would emphasize the extent to which every baboon mother is a "dual-career mother" spending most of each day "making a living": feeding, walking, avoiding predation, while also caring for her infant.

Acutely sensitive to the problem of observer bias, Jeanne Altmann developed techniques for choosing subjects at random. She made sure each individual was watched for the same number of minutes. Then she used statistical tests to analyze the results. It was the best available antidote to the all-too-human habit of seeing only what we expect to see. In time, such methods for studying free-ranging animals became standard practice for animal behaviorists, and spread into human behavioral ecology. Instead of relying on asking mothers what they remembered doing, or thought they should do, accurate accounts of what mothers were actually doing became available.

Multiple Roles for Mom

"In all aspects of the present study one fact recurs: baboon mothers, like most primate mothers, including humans, are dual-career mothers in a complex ecological and social setting," Altmann wrote. "They do not take care of their infants while isolated in small houses or cages, as the rest of baboon life goes on. They are an integral part of that life and must continue to function within it. The baboon world affects them, and they it, through their lifetime." With 70 percent of their day going toward making a living, and perhaps another 10 to 15 percent for resting, these baboon mothers were pushing the envelope of their own survival. If they were to breed any faster, they would risk maternal depletion and death.

Altmann's field research shifted the focus away from what had become an overemphasis on male-male competition and mate choice back to natural selection. In balancing her tradeoffs so as to stay alive and breed, almost every aspect of a mother's life was shaped by natural selection.

At the same time, Altmann was managing her own balancing act, raising two children and doing science under harsh field conditions. She also had another concern. The study of mother-infant relations was at that time still widely viewed as the "home economics" of animal behavior, an area of little theoretical significance. Altmann feared that her hard work would not be taken seriously. Instead, her 1980 monograph *Baboon Mothers and Infants* became a classic in the study of life-history tradeoffs.

Varying Strategies

A female's lifetime reproductive success (or fitness) depends on luck, of course—everything does—and, as in the case of Altmann's baboons, on the physical constraints of the environment. In an evolutionary sense, how one mother fares relative to another depends on how well she handles the series of tradeoffs she encounters in the course of her entire life. One tradeoff is between growing larger and maintaining herself (somatic effort) versus reproductive effort. The second main tradeoff involves how she allocates bodily resources available for reproduction among offspring. Again, there is a quantity-versus-quality tradeoff. In some species, such as rabbits and galagos, mothers invest little in each infant and breed fast; others, like a chimpanzee or a human, breed slowly over a long life. Others pursue mixed strategies, alternating according to conditions.

Golden hamsters, quintessentially flexible breeders adapted to the irregular rainfall and erratic food supplies of their arid Middle

Eastern environment, illustrate the art of iteroparity—or, how to breed successfully more than once over a lifetime. In addition to building a nest, licking her pups clean, protecting and suckling them—all pleasantly maternal-seeming pursuits—a mother hamster may also recoup some of her investment in these pups by eating a few, a time-honored maternal tactic for adjusting litter size in line with prevailing conditions. Among mice, mothers actually cull so as to enhance litter quality (favoring the heaviest pups) or to adjust the size of the litter. Occasionally, they abandon whole litters if the number of pups born falls below an acceptable threshold, something large mammals like lions and bears will also do.

Once embarked upon a reproductive trajectory, mothers face new challenges. How to reconcile conflicting demands of different offspring? Treat each offspring as equivalent, or value some over others? Should a mother gamble on an offspring now or reserve herself for some future offspring who might be born under more promising conditions, or might perhaps be born a sex that is more advantageous for her to rear? Given that her body is deteriorating over time, when should she throw in the towel, quit producing, and care for her daughter's offspring instead?

Big Momma

When was it worthwhile to delay reproduction and keep growing? Zoologist Katherine Ralls hypothesized that a big mother could be a better mother. The standard answer to why males are bigger than females is sexual selection: males are elected to be bigger and stronger than rival males. Females remain smaller, the ecologically optimal size for their environment—a sort of default body size. During the 1970s, Ralls challenged the fixation with sexual selection. Playing devil's advocate, she listed all the mammals in which *females grow larger than males*, an eclectic array of moon rats, musk shrews, chinchillas, jackrabbits, cottontails, klipspringers, duikers, water chevrotains, dik-diks, marmosets, bats, bats, and more bats, and so forth, and then showed how poorly sexual selection theory accounted for many of the cases.

Increasing fecundity with body mass turns out to be one of the main reasons so many invertebrates, such as spiders, have females larger than their mates. Among species where mothers produce more eggs or young as they grow older and bigger (the best examples are fish), females seem to live on and on until something external kills them. Both fishermen and male fish seek out these "big mothers"—the former for their cachet, the latter for their greater fecundity. Depending on the species, big mothers produce bigger babies, deliver larger quantities of rich milk more quickly (as whales do), outcompete smaller females so as to monopolize resources available in their group, or, as spotted hyena females must do, not only defend their place in the chow line but also defend their infants from carnivorous and extremely cannibalistic group mates. The fact that bigger mothers make better mothers probably explains why the blue whale female grows to 196 tons, qualifying her as the largest mammal in the world.

Ancestral Humans

Even among the anthropoid apes, and in spite of a venerable history of sexually selected males being bigger than females, Ralls's "big mother hypothesis" helps to explain the emergence around 1.7 million years ago of a hominid species with females closer in size to that of males. There was a dramatic *decrease* in the degree of sexual dimorphism (size difference between males and females) in these animals. *Homo erectus* males and females were about the same size as humans today, and were just embarking on the lifestyle characterized by a division of labor between male hunters and female gatherers. To understand why *Homo erectus* females, as well as females belonging to the closely related species *Homo ergaster*, grew twice as large as australopithecine females—of which the famous fossil known as "Lucy" is the best known—we need to consider selection pressures *on mothers.*

Whereas Lucy's mate would have been 50 percent again larger than she was, Missus Erectus's fellow was a mere 20 percent bigger than she was, around the same order of magnitude as the 15 percent or so difference in body size that characterizes men and women in modern populations. In other words, both males and females grew larger; but by 1.7 million years ago, with the emergence of *Homo erectus*, selection pressures favoring larger body size became more important for females than for males. Why was this so? For a hunter there may be a ceiling on just how large he can grow and still be effective in the pursuit of game. Ultimately, though, speculates University of California, Davis, paleontologist Henry McHenry, the decline in size difference between the two sexes had to do with big moms making better moms.

Bigger May Be Better

Once hominid mothers became more terrestrial and traveled farther afield from their usual escape routes (into trees), were big
moms better able to defend themselves and their babies? Were
they superior foragers, able to push aside big boulders to get at un-
derground tubers? Better able to accommodate larger babies pass-
ing through the birth canal, and, after birth, to carry large, slow-
maturing babies long distances? The bigger a mother is, for
example, the more efficiently she manages a heavy burden while
striding along two-legged.

Listening to paleontologists ponder these questions today, I think
back to the early 1970s, when in order to hear Katherine Ralls lecture I would trek to the other side of Harvard Square, far from the
Biology Labs (where mainstream evolution was taught), to the
Radcliffe Institute—at that time a unique forum for women scholars. Ralls's enthusiasm for the "big mother hypothesis" was infectious. I can still recall the undisguised glee with which Ralls (who
like me is tall) used to rattle off World Health Organization statistics on the correlation between height and easier, safer childbirth.
Other times, a Jeremiah-like touch of exasperation would enter her
voice. "It's so obvious, why don't they see . . ." how much more to
the story there is than male-male competition and sexual selection!

Female Chimps' Strategies

By the end of the twentieth century, the role of Flo, Jane Goodall's
most endearing mother chimp, was expanded and recast. Flo's evident tenderness and patience are only part of the story about her
success as a mother. If in this selection I fail to stress sufficiently
this nurturing component, the reason is that I assume it is already
well known, widely described, and commonly assumed. But there
are secrets to Flo's reproductive success that are less well known,
less often noted. These include Flo's ability to carve out for herself a secure and productive territory deep within the boundaries
patrolled by the Gombe males. Many of these males were former
sexual consorts; others were her own sons who had risen to a high
rank in the fluctuating local hierarchy. Flo was as secure as a female chimp could be from outside males who from time to time
would raid her community and, if they could, kill not just unrelated infants but adult males and older females as well.

Researchers study the behaviors of chimpanzees to learn more about the dominant role that the female plays in their species.

But Flo did more than commandeer a productive larder and keep her offspring safe. She supported her offspring politically, permitting Fifi to translate her mother's advantages into her own. At Flo's death, Fifi parlayed her mother's local connections into the inestimable privilege of philopatry, remaining in her natal place. Philopatry (which means literally "loving one's home country") meant that instead of migrating away to find a new place to live, Fifi—like half of all females born at Gombe—managed to stay where she was born. Fifi continued to use her mother's rich, familiar larder, and enjoy the protection of male kin.

Make no mistake: reproductively, nothing becomes a female more than remaining among kin. Thus advantaged, Fifi began breeding at an unusually early age, and so far has produced seven successive offspring, six surviving—the all-time record for lifetime reproductive success in a wild Great Ape female. She also holds the record for shortest interval between surviving births ever reported in wild chimps. Her second-born son, Frodo, has grown into the largest male on record at Gombe and ranks in the status hierarchy just below the current alpha male, Fifi's firstborn son,

Freud, while Fanni, Fifi's third-born, holds the record for the earliest ever anogenital swelling [indicating sexual maturity], at 8.5 years. Thus does Flo's family prosper.

Deadly Dominance

Early on, Goodall and her students noticed that when Flo approached other females they gave nervous pant-grunts and moved out of her way. Females could be divided into those that held sway and those that gave way. What Goodall did not immediately grasp, however, was why female rank was so important. We now know that, *given the opportunity*, a more dominant female chimp will kill and eat babies born to other females.

Over the decades that records were kept at Gombe, at least four, possibly as many as ten, newborn infants were killed by females. When Goodall reported the first two cases of infant killing and cannibalism by another mother in 1977, the so-called crimes of a female named Passion, she, like most people, assumed that the female killing these infants must be deranged. A few sociobiologists suspected otherwise and suggested that females from a more dominant lineage were "eliminating a competitor while the infant was still sufficiently vulnerable to be dispatched with impunity."

From the 1970s onward, isolated cases of infanticide by rival mothers continued to be reported for other species of social mammals—ground squirrels, prairie dogs, wild dogs, marmosets, some fifty species in all. Most cases were attributed to either a mineral deficiency or protein lust by a hungry female (since in some cases victims were eaten) or to mothers clearing out a niche and thereby making resources available for her own breeding efforts—a model first proposed by sociobiologist Paul Sherman at Cornell University. As more evidence became available, "the crimes of passion" were looking more deliberate than anomalous, and in species like chimps, other females were a hazard that mothers had to watch out for.

Safety in Status

Nevertheless, chimpanzees breed so slowly that it was 1997 before Goodall and zoologist Anne Pusey had collected enough data to show a statistically significant correlation between female rank and a mother's ability to keep her infants alive. This finding caused them to reevaluate their longstanding diagnosis of Passion's "pathological" behavior. When, two decades after the first cases were reported, Fifi's daughter attacked the daughter of a subordinate female, Pusey assumed it was a failed attempt at infanticide.

Mother chimps like Flo, then, were not simply doting nurturers but entrepreneurial dynasts as well. A female's quest for status—her ambition, if you will—has become inseparable from her ability to keep her offspring and grand-offspring alive. Far from conflicting with maternity, such a female's "ambitious" tendencies are part and parcel of maternal success.

Subtle Female Competition

Darwin had set up a revolutionary new framework for understanding the behavior unfolding before us in the natural world, but it took another century to expand that paradigm to include the full range of selection pressures on both sexes. One reason it took so long to fully assess the female side of the equation was that competition between females tends to be more subtle than the boisterous, often violent, roaring and bellowing of males. Female mammals tend to confine overt competition to the spheres that actually matter in terms of status and their ability to produce high-quality offspring.

Several changes contributed to the new awareness or reproductive variation among mothers. In addition to the theoretical shift to focus on individuals, field studies were lasting longer, decades rather than months. Also, more women were doing field research. In 1875 Antoinette Brown Blackwell had lamented that "Only a woman can approach [evolution] from a feminine standpoint and there are none but beginners among us in this class of investigations." A century later, 37 percent of Ph.D.s in biology in the United States were being awarded to women, and the proportion in the field of animal behavior was about the same. Although male and female researchers do science the same way, they may be attracted to different problems. The upshot of all these factors was that this time, when distaff Darwinians tapped male evolutionists on the shoulder, many of the latter were primed to respond.

Undoing Male Bias

By the late 1980s, prominent male biologists were joining their women colleagues in pointing out the need to correct "inadvertent machismo" in their respective fields. Some of them made points similar to those [feminist writers George] Eliot, Blackwell, and [Clémence] Royer had tried to communicate more than a century earlier. "Research in biology," renowned entomologist William Eberhard noted, "has traditionally been carried out mainly by men rather than by women, and it is possible that, as has happened in the social sciences, research may sometimes be inadvertently influenced by male-centered outlooks.

Wherever the evolution of reproductive strategies was studied, the importance of taking into account the reproductive interests of all players involved—female or male, adult or immature—was increasingly recognized. Whether in entomology, primatology, ornithology, or human behavioral ecology, researchers rushed—like prospectors in a gold rush—to seek the mother lode of new insight to be had from incorporating females' as well as males' perspectives into their research.

Scientific observation of animals living in their natural environments during the last decades of the twentieth century yielded a far more dynamic and multifaceted portrait of female nature than anything previously imagined. Most surprising were all the ways that mothers influence their offspring's development through both genetic (including female choice) and nongenetic effects. The updated image of old Flo, for example, allows us a glimpse into the significance of such "maternal effects." Fifi, Flo's daughter, entered the world advantaged by her mother's rank, a maternal effect that pointed to ever more subtle ways—beyond genetically inherited attributes and succor—through which mothers influence the fates of their offspring. By the end of the twentieth century, the spotlight shifted so as to begin to illuminate in rigorous and controlled studies how organisms develop in specific contexts. Development would turn out to be the critical missing link in evolutionary thinking.

Evolutionary Medicine

By Randolph M. Nesse and George C. Williams

As Randolph M. Nesse and George C. Williams explain in the following selection, evolutionary (or Darwinian) medicine takes a long view of the human body and its biological enemies. Our bodies, the authors explain, have some features better adapted to the way our ancestors lived than to our modern lifestyles, and have other features that are still "catching up" to the extended life expectancies we enjoy. Darwinian medicine not only provides insights into such features but also strategies for treating ailments that arise from them. Randolph M. Nesse is a physician who also serves as a professor in the University of Michigan Medical School. George C. Williams is professor emeritus of ecology and evolution at New York's State University at Stony Brook. He won renown in 1966 for focusing the attention of the evolutionary studies community on the central role of the gene in natural selection.

Why isn't the body more reliable? Why is there disease at all?. . . First, there are genes that make us vulnerable to disease. Some—though fewer than has been thought—are defectives continually arising from new mutations but kept scarce by natural selection. Other genes cannot be eliminated because they cause no disadvantages until it is too late in life for them to affect fitness. Most deleterious genetic effects, however, are actively maintained by selection because they have unappreciated benefits that outweigh their costs. Some of these are maintained because of heterozygote advantage; some are selected because they increase their own frequency, despite creating a disadvantage for the individual who bears them; some are genetic quirks that have adverse effects only when they interact with a novel environmental factor.

Second, disease results from exposure to novel factors that were not present in the environment in which we evolved. Given enough time, the body can adapt to almost anything, but the ten thousand years since the beginnings of civilization are not nearly enough time, and we suffer accordingly. Infectious agents evolve so fast that our defenses are always a step behind. Third, disease results from design compromises, such as upright posture with its associated back problems. Fourth, we are not the only species with adaptations produced and maintained by natural selection, which works just as hard for pathogens trying to eat us and the organisms we want to eat. In conflicts with these organisms, as in baseball, you can't win 'em all. Finally, disease results from unfortunate historical legacies. If the organism had been designed with the possibility of fresh starts and major changes, there would be better ways of preventing many diseases. Alas, every successive generation of the human body must function well, with no chance to go back and start afresh.

The human body turns out to be both fragile and robust. Like all products of organic evolution, it is a bundle of compromises, each of which offers an advantage, but often at the price of susceptibility to disease. These susceptibilities cannot be eliminated by any duration of natural selection, for it is the very power of natural selection that created them. . . .

Take something . . . more chronic and complicated, plantar fasciitis. More often known as heel spurs, this common disorder causes intense pain on the inside edge of the heel, especially first thing in the morning. The proximate cause is inflammation at the point where the heel attaches to the plantar fascia, a band of tough tissue that connects the front and rear of the foot like the string on a bow, supporting the arch of the foot. With every footstep it stretches, bearing the weight of the body thousands of times every day. Why does this fascia fail so often? The easy answer is that natural selection cannot shape a tissue strong enough to do the job—but by now this explanation should be suspect. Somewhat more plausible is the possibility that we began walking on two feet so recently that there has not been enough time for natural selection to strengthen the fascia sufficiently. The problem with this explanation is that plantar fasciitis is common and crippling. Like nearsightedness, it would, in the natural environment, so drastically decrease fitness that it would be strongly selected against. Some experts say plantar fasciitis arises in people who walk with their toes pointed out, a conformation that puts increased stress on the tissue. But then why do we walk that way? Is it the modern habit of wearing shoes? But many people who have never worn shoes also walk with their toes pointed outward.

Chair-Bound

Two clues suggest that plantar fasciitis may result from environmental novelty. First, exercises that stretch the plantar fascia to make it longer and more resilient are effective in relieving the problem. Second, many of us do something hunter-gatherers don't: we sit in chairs all day. Most hunter-gatherers walk for hours each day, instead of compressing their exercise into an efficient aerobic workout. When they aren't walking, they don't use chairs, they squat, a position that steadily stretches the plantar fascia. No plantar fasciitis and physical therapy for them, just squatting and walking for hours each day. This hypothesis, that plantar fasciitis results from prolonged sitting that allows the fascia to contract and that the disorder can be prevented and relieved by squatting and other stretching of the fascia, can readily be tested with epidemiological data and straightforward treatment studies.

Another good challenge for Darwinian medicine is the current controversy about whether it is wise to take antioxidants such as vitamin C, vitamin E, and beta-carotene. Folklore has long credited these agents with reducing heart disease, cancer, and even the effects of aging. Controlled studies are increasingly supporting these claims, especially for the prevention of atherosclerosis, although a major study in 1994 reported that beta-carotene appeared to *increase* the risk of cancer in some people. The agents are still deemed controversial, and many physicians studying them recommend caution until larger studies can assess their risks as well as benefits. We agree with this general conservatism but hope that an evolutionary view can speed the process. . . . Natural selection seems to have resulted in high levels of several of the body's own antioxidants even though they cause disease. Uric acid levels are higher in species that live longer and are so high in humans that we are susceptible to gout. It appears that natural selection has acted to increase the human levels of uric acid, superoxide dismutase, and perhaps bilirubin and other substances as well, because they are antioxidants that slow some effects of aging in a species that has greatly increased its life span in just the past few hundred thousand years.

Why doesn't the body have antioxidant levels that are already optimal? It is possible that our antiaging mechanisms are still catching up with the recent increase in our life span. It is also possible that the costs of high levels of antioxidants (perhaps decreases in our resistance to infection or toxins?) have restricted them to levels that were optimal for a normal Stone Age lifetime of thirty or forty years. These possibilities suggest that adding extra antioxidants to the diet may have benefits that exceed the costs. In contrast to the many cases in which an evolutionary view argues against excessive intervention, here it supports the active pursuit of strategies that may prevent some effects of aging. A major part of such studies should be a search for other antioxidants in the body and an assessment of their costs and benefits. It would be interesting to see if people with high uric acid levels have costs other than gout and whether they show fewer signs of aging than other people. It will also be important to look for similar costs and benefits in our primate relatives. With this knowledge we will be in a better position to decide who will benefit from taking antioxidants and what the side effects might be.

Making Theory into Practice

Asking biochemists or epidemiologists to judge proposals to test evolutionary hypotheses is like asking mineral chemists to judge proposals on continental drift. Darwinian medicine needs its own funding panels staffed by reviewers who know the concepts and methods of evolutionary biology. Realistically, the prospects are poor for major government funding soon. The best hope for rapid growth of the field lies in the vision of private donors or foundations that could create institutes to support the development of Darwinian medicine. Even moderate support of this sort could quickly change the course of medicine, just as prior investments in biochemical and genetic research are now transforming our lives. As [biologist] René Dubos noted in 1965:

> In many ways, the present situation of organismic biology and especially of environmental medicine is very similar to that of the physicochemical sciences related to medicine around 1900. At that time there was no place in the United States dedicated to the pursuit of physicochemical biology, and the scholars who were interested in this field were treated as second-class citizens in the med-

ical community. Fortunately, a few philanthropists were made aware of this situation, and they endowed new kinds of research facilities to change the trend. The Rockefeller Institute is probably the most typical example of a conscious and successful attempt to provide a basis of physicochemical knowledge for the art of medicine. . . . Organismic and especially environmental medicine constitute today virgin territories even less developed than was physicochemical biology 50 years ago. They will remain undeveloped unless a systematic effort is made to give them academic recognition and to provide adequate facilities for their exploration.

Latecomer

Why has it taken more than a hundred years to apply Darwin's theory systematically to disease? Historians of science will eventually address this question but from this close perspective several explanations seem likely: the supposed difficulty in formulating and testing evolutionary hypotheses about disease, the recency of some advances in evolutionary biology, and some peculiarities of the field of medicine.

Biologists have long tried to figure out the evolutionary origins and functions for organismic characteristics, but it has taken a surprisingly long time to realize that this enterprise is fundamentally different from trying to figure out the structure of organisms and how they work. Harvard biologist Ernst Mayr, in *The Growth of Biological Thought*, traces the parallel development of the two biologies. Medicine, while at the forefront of proximate biology, has been curiously late in addressing evolutionary questions. This is, no doubt, in part simply because the questions and goals are so different. It takes a wrenching shift to stop asking why an individual has a particular disease and to ask instead what characteristics of a species make all of its members susceptible to that disease. It has seemed a bit odd until now even to ask how something maladaptive like disease might have been shaped by natural selection. Furthermore, medicine is a practical enterprise, and it hasn't been immediately obvious how evolutionary explanations might help us prevent or treat disease. We hope this [selection] convinces many people that seeking evolutionary explanations for disease is both possible and of substantial practical value.

If we are to assign blame for the tardiness of medicine in making use of relevant ideas in evolutionary biology, it rests as much with evolutionary biologists as with the medical profession. It took evolutionists an inexcusably long time to formulate the relevant ideas. Given the powerful insights of Darwin, [Alfred Russel] Wallace, and a few others in the middle of the nineteenth century, and the Mendelian revolution in genetics in the early years of the twentieth, why was it not until [Ronald A.] Fisher's book of 1930 that we had the first fruitful idea about why the number of boys and girls born is nearly equal? Why was it not until [Peter B.] Medawar's midcentury work that we had any idea why there is such a thing as senescence? Why was it not until [William D.] Hamilton's publications in 1964 that there was any realization that kinship would have some relevance to evolution? Why was it not until the 1970s and 1980s that we had useful ideas on how parasites and hosts, or plants and herbivores, influence each other's evolution? We believe that the answers to these and related questions will be found in a persistent antipathy to evolutionary ideas in general and to adaptation and natural selection in particular (even among some biologists). Meanwhile, we will simply note that medical researchers can hardly be blamed for failing to use the ideas of other sorts of scientists before those scientists developed them.

The Reluctance of the Medical Establishment

Medical scientists may also hesitate to consider functional hypotheses because of their indoctrination in the experimental method. Most of them were taught early, firmly—and wrongly—that science progresses only by means of experiment. But many scientific advances begin with a theory, and much testing of hypotheses does not rely on the experimental method. Geology, for instance, cannot replay the history of the earth, but it nonetheless can reach firm conclusions about how basins and ranges got that way. Like evolutionary hypotheses, geological hypotheses are tested by explaining available evidence and by predicting new findings that have not yet been sought in the existing record.

Finally, medicine, like other branches of science, is especially wary of ideas that in any way resemble recently overcome mistakes. Medicine fought for years to exclude vitalism, the idea that organisms were imbued with a mysterious "life force," so it continues to attack anything that is even vaguely similar. Likewise, *teleology* of a naive and erroneous sort keeps reappearing and must be expelled. Many people recollect from freshman philosophy class that teleology is the mistake of trying to explain something on the basis of its purpose or goal. This admonition is wise if it establishes an awareness that future conditions cannot influence the present. It is unwise if it also implies that present plans for the future cannot affect present processes and, through them, future conditions. Present plans may include printed recipes for baking cakes or the information in the DNA of bird's eggs. Functional explanations in biology imply not future influences on the present but a prolonged cycling of reproduction and selection. A bird embryo develops wing rudiments in the egg because earlier individuals that failed to do so left no descendants. Adult birds lay eggs in which embryos develop wing rudiments for the same reason. In this sense, a bird's wing rudiments are preparation for its future but are caused by its past history. Evolutionary explanations based on a trait's function do not imply that evolution involves any consciousness, active planning, or goal-directedness. While medicine is wise to be on guard against sliding back into discredited teleological reasoning, this wariness has prevented it from taking full advantage of the solid advances in mainstream evolutionary science. Through its efforts to keep from being dragged back, medicine has, paradoxically, been left behind.

Changes in Education

Medical education is similarly in trouble because of trying to guard against the old mistakes. The origins of its current quandary lie in the solution to a previous one. Early in [the twentieth] century, the Carnegie Foundation sponsored an extensive investigation of medical education by Abraham Flexner. In his cross-country travels, he reported a haphazard system of medical apprenticeship in which physicians, good and bad, took on assistants who, one way or another, learned something about medicine. Doctors' formal study of basic science was sporadic, and even their knowledge of basic anatomy and physiology was inconsistent. The Flexner report, published in 1910, formed the basis of new accreditation standards that required medical schools to provide future physicians with a foundation in basic science.

On this count, medical schools have far exceeded Flexner's hopes. In fact, one wonders what Flexner would say if he could see today's medical curricula. Now medical students are not only exposed to basic sciences, they are inundated with the latest advances by teachers who are subspecialist basic science researchers. At curriculum meetings in every medical school there are battles for students' time and minds. The microbiologists want more lab time, the anatomists want more too. The pathologists feel they cannot possibly fit their material into a mere forty hours of lecture. The pharmacologists say they will continue flunking 30 percent of the class until they get enough time to cover all the new drugs. The epidemiologists and biochemists and physiologists and psychiatrists and neuroscience experts all want more time, and certainly the students must keep up with the latest advances in genetics. Then they need to learn enough statistics and scientific methodology to be able to read the research literature. And they must somehow learn, before they start their work on the wards, how to talk with patients, how to do a physical exam, how to write up a patient report, how to draw blood, do a culture, a spinal tap, a Pap smear, measure eyeball pressure, examine urine and blood, and, and . . . The amounts of knowledge and the lists of tasks are overwhelming, but all must be completed in the first two years of medical school.

Making Room for Darwin

How is all this possible? It isn't. Why set impossible expectations? In part because we naively want our physicians to know everything. Another reason, however, is that no one person is in charge. When a committee decides on the class schedule and every basic science wants more time, the solution is to go on increasing the total amount of class time. Thirty or more hours each week in class is not unusual. After that, the students go home to study their textbooks and notes.

One might think that students' complaints would lead to reform, but decades of polite complaints changed little. It was technology that finally precipitated some change, technology in the form of the photocopy machine. Instead of going to class, students hire one person to take notes for each lecture, then all of them receive copies. It turns out to be a better survival strategy to stay home and study the notes than to go to class. When only twenty students attend a class for two hundred, professors hit the roof and curriculum reform is born. New attempts are being made, under the strong leadership of some deans, to cut back on the hours, reduce the amount of material, find new ways to transmit it. If these efforts succeed, it will be wonderful indeed.

Such efforts might even make room for Darwinian medicine, except that there are no Departments of Evolutionary Medicine to advocate inclusion of this material and few medical faculty members who know the material and want to teach it. It will take time and further leadership from medical school deans to make room in the medical curriculum for an introduction to the basic science of evolution and its applications in medicine. When evolution is included, it will give students not only a new perspective on disease but also an integrating framework on which to hang a million otherwise arbitrary facts. Darwinian medicine could bring intellectual coherence to the chaotic enterprise of medical education.

In the Doctor's Office

While many clinical implications of an evolutionary view await future research, others can immediately transform the way patients and doctors see disease. Let us listen in as first a pre-Darwinian and then a post-Darwinian physician talk to a patient about gout.

"So, Doctor, it is gout that has my big toe flaming, is it? What causes gout?"

"Gout is caused by crystals of uric acid in the joint fluid. I expect you can imagine only too well how some gritty crystals could make a joint painful."

"So why do I have it and you don't?"

"Some people have high levels of uric acid in their systems, probably because of some combination of genes and diet."

"So why isn't the body designed better? You would think there would be some system to keep uric acid levels lower."

"Well, we can't expect the body to be perfect, now, can we?"

At this point our pre-Darwinian physician gives up on science and dodges the question, implying that such "why" questions need not be taken seriously. Most likely, he or she doesn't recognize the distinction between proximate and evolutionary explanations, to say nothing of the importance and legitimacy of evolutionary explanations for disease.

The Darwinian physician gives a different answer, one closer to what the patient wanted and was entitled to.

"That's a good question. It turns out that human uric acid levels are much higher than those of other primates and that uric acid levels in a species are correlated with its life span. The longer-lived the species, the higher the uric acid levels. It seems that uric acid protects our cells against damage from oxidation, one of the causes of aging. So natural selection probably selected for higher uric acid levels in our ancestors, even though some people end up getting gout, because those higher levels are especially useful in a species that lives as long as we do."

"So high levels of uric acid prevent aging!"

"Basically, that seems to be right. So far, however, there is no evidence that individuals with high uric acid levels live an especially long time, and in any case you don't want your toe to stay like that, so we are going to go ahead and get your uric acid levels down to the normal range to get the gout under control."

"Sounds sensible to me, Doc."

Other Applications

This is not an isolated example. A Darwinian perspective can already assist in the management of many medical conditions. Take strep throat:

"Well, it's strep all right, so you will need to take some penicillin for seven days," says the Darwinian physician.

"That will make me better faster, right?" the patient says hoarsely.

"Probably, and it will also make it less likely that you will develop disease like rheumatic fever because of your body making immune substances that attack the bacteria."

"But why doesn't my body know better than to make substances that will attack my own heart?"

"Well, the streptococcus has evolved along with humans for millions of years, and its trick is to imitate the codes of human cells. So when we make antibodies that attack the strep bacteria, those antibodies are prone to attack our own tissues as well. We are in a contest with the strep organism, but we can't win because the strep evolves much faster than we do. It has a new generation every hour or so, while we take twenty years. Thank goodness we can still kill it with antibiotics, although this may be a temporary blessing. You will do yourself and the rest of the world a favor by taking your antibiotics even after you feel better, because otherwise you may be giving a lift to those variants that can survive short exposures to antibiotics, and those antibiotic-resistant organisms make life difficult for us all."

"Oh, now I see why I have to take the whole bottle. Okay."

Or take a patient who has had a heart attack:

"So, Doctor, if my high cholesterol is caused by my genes, what good will it do to change my diet?"

"Well, those genes aren't harmful in the normal environment we evolved in. If you spent six or eight hours walking around each day to find food, and if most of your food was complex starches and very lean meat from wild game, you wouldn't get heart disease."

"But how come I crave exactly the foods you say I shouldn't eat? No potato chips, no ice cream, no cheese, no steak? You medical types want to take away all the foods that taste best."

"I'm afraid we were wired to seek out certain things that were essential in small amounts but scarce on the African savannah. When our ancestors found a source of salt, sugar, or fat, it was usually a good idea for them to eat all they could get. Now that we can easily get any amount of salt, sugar, or fat just by tossing things into the grocery cart, most of us eat more than twice as much fat as our ancestors did, and lots more salt and sugar. You are right, it is a kind of a cruel joke—we do want exactly those things that are bad for us. Eating a healthy diet does not come naturally in the modern environment. We have to use our brains and our willpower to compensate for our primitive urges."

"Well, I still don't like giving up my favorite foods, but at least that makes it understandable."

Limitations

There are a hundred more examples: advice given to a patient with a cold or diarrhea; an explanation of aging; the significance of morning sickness during pregnancy; the possible utility of allergy. While most medical conditions have yet to be explored from an evolutionary view, Darwinian medicine can already be useful in the clinic.

A caveat is necessary. Doctors and patients, like all other people, are prone to extend theories too far. We have lost count of how many reporters have called asking, "So you're saying we should not take aspirin for a fever, right?" Wrong! Clinical principles of medicine should come from clinical research, not from theory. It is a mistake to avoid aspirin just because we know that fever can be useful, and a mistake not to treat the unpleasant symptoms of some cases of pregnancy, sickness, allergy, and anxiety. Each condition needs to be studied separately and each case considered individually. An evolutionary approach does, however, suggest that many such treatments are unnecessary or harmful and that we should do the research to see if the benefits are worth the costs.

Moral Dimensions

We have said before, but here repeat, that moral principles cannot be deduced from biological facts. For instance, the knowledge that aging and death are inevitable has no direct implications for how much of our medical dollar we should spend on the very elderly. Facts can, however, help us to achieve whatever goals we decide to strive for. The current crisis in funding and organization of health care in the United States comes from several sources, including new funding mechanisms, new technology, other economic changes, and social values that increasingly condemn gross differences in the quality of health care. In a system this complex, no general policies will please everyone, and it may not be possible to implement the best available policies because of the power of politics.

While not pretending to offer solutions, we observe that the many participants in this debate don't even agree on what disease is. They know disease is bad but differ wildly on where it comes from and the extent to which it can be prevented or relieved. Some blame faulty genes, others emphasize the amount of disease that results from unfortunate human predilections, especially poor diets and drug use. According to one recent authoritative article, more than 70 percent of morbidity and mortality in the United States is preventable. The article argues strongly for investing in prevention because it will pay off in reduced health care costs. What a terrible irony and frightening harbinger it is that such a noble and practical proposal to improve human health has to be couched as a way to save money! In the light of history, however, this approach is understandable. Again and again, panels of distinguished physicians and researchers have called for prevention instead of treatment. The field of preventive medicine now provides some help, especially in matters of public policy, but people still do not get reliable advice from their physicians about how to stay healthy. New ways of organizing medical care may finally provide incentives for dedicating substantial clinical resources to preserving health based on principles of Darwinian medicine.

CHRONOLOGY

510 B.C.

The approximate year of the birth of Anaximander, an early Greek philosopher whose speculations on the diversity of life foreshadow the theory of evolution.

384 B.C.

The Greek philosopher Aristotle is born. He takes a staunch position against the concept that species evolve into other species.

A.D. 1707

Carl Linnaeus, the "father of taxonomy," is born in Sweden. Although he trains and practices as a physician, he gains lasting fame for systematically categorizing thousands of living beings.

1769

The founder of modern paleontology, Georges Cuvier, is born. As a professor at France's National Museum of Natural History, he demonstrates that many fossils represent extinct animal lineages. Ironically, he remains opposed to the idea that species evolve.

1797

Charles Lyell, revolutionary geologist and close friend of Charles Darwin's, is born in Scotland. Though at first opposed to evolution, Lyell establishes "uniformatarianism" as a basic principle of geology, opening the way for Darwin to consider immense periods of time in which evolution can do its work.

1803

Erasmus Darwin, grandfather of Charles Darwin, publishes *Zoonomia*, a book that contains many speculations on life prefiguring his grandson's theory.

1809

Charles Darwin, the founder of scientific evolutionary theory, is born; French naturalist Jean-Baptiste Lamarck publishes his somewhat confused theory of evolution in a book called *Philosophie Zoologique.* It incorrectly suggests that characteristics acquired through experience can be passed down to offspring.

1823

Alfred Russel Wallace, a naturalist whose career and thinking parallel Darwin's, is born in rural England.

1830

Lyell publishes the first volume of his *Principles of Geology,* in which he interprets earth history as a process of gradual changes caused by unchanging natural laws.

1831

Darwin sails as an unpaid naturalist on the HMS *Beagle* on what will become an around-the-world voyage of discovery.

1835

The *Beagle* reaches the Galápagos Islands, where Darwin collects unique specimens that will later help him to formulate his theory.

1836

After five years at sea, the *Beagle* returns to England.

1837

Darwin donates his specimens to London's Zoological Society. His thirteen species of Galápagos finches become the focus of intense study, prompting Darwin's thoughts in the direction of evolution.

1842

Darwin writes his first essay on evolution, including the concept of natural selection, but decides to keep it secret.

1855

Wallace, while exploring in the Malay Peninsula, writes an essay on the natural laws of speciation.

1858

In an arrangement brokered by Lyell, Darwin, and Wallace each have a paper on natural selection presented in their absence at the Linnean Society in London. This marks the first time Darwin's theory is published.

1859

On the Origin of Species, Darwin's most famous work, is published and rapidly becomes an influential bestseller.

1860

Naturalist Thomas Henry Huxley and Church of England bishop Samuel Wilberforce engage in a famous debate at Oxford University on Darwin's theory of evolution.

1866

Monk Gregor Mendel publishes a little-noticed paper on his study of heredity in peas. His research eventually becomes the foundation of genetics, but Darwin never comes to learn about it.

1871

Charles Darwin publishes his book, *The Descent of Man and Selection in Relation to Sex.*

1876

Botanist Asa Gray, America's leading advocate of Darwin's work, publishes an influential book of essays on evolutionary theory called *Darwiniana.*

1882

Darwin dies and is buried next to Sir Isaac Newton in London's Westminster Abbey.

1921

Lawyer and politician William Jennings Bryan publishes a pamphlet called *The Menace of Darwinism.* He calls for taxpayers to have the right to decide what is taught in science classes.

1925

In Tennessee teacher John Scopes is charged with violating state law by teaching evolution. In the so-called Scopes Monkey Trial, trial lawyer Clarence Darrow defends Scopes, while Bryan joins the prosecution team. At the trial's end, Scopes is convicted; Bryan collapses and dies.

1930

With the publication of his book *The Genetical Theory of Natural Selection*, biological statistics expert Ronald Fisher launches an effort to move evolution onto a more empirical foundation through population genetics.

1932

British geneticist J.B.S. Haldane advances the "modern synthesis" of evolution and genetics with the publication of his book *The Causes of Evolution.*

1950

In an encyclical titled *Humani Generis*, Pope Pius XII states that evolution does not necessarily conflict with Christianity.

1953

Francis Crick and James Watson publish a paper that correctly identifies the double-helix structure of DNA, opening the way for biologists to study evolution by identifying and tracking genes.

1957

British biologist H.B.D. Kettlewell publishes a famous study of peppered moth populations in England. He finds that industrial pollution has darkened the lichens on which the moths roost, leading to an increase in the proportion of dark-colored moths at the expense of light-colored moths.

1968

Sewall Wright, a biologist whose concept of "fitness landscapes" transforms the depiction of evolution, publishes *Evolution and the Genetics of Populations.*

1972

Paleontologists Stephen Jay Gould and Niles Eldredge publish a paper claiming that they have discovered a stop-and-go alternative to Darwin's evolutionary gradualism. They call it "punctuated equilibrium."

1975

Biologist Edward O. Wilson launches a new branch of evolutionary studies with the publication of *Sociobiology*, which applies evolutionary principles to explain human social behavior.

1978

In a long-term study on finches in the Galápagos Islands, teams of researchers led by Peter and Rosemary Grant become the first to systematically document natural selection at work in a population.

1987

The U.S. Supreme Court rules in *Edwards v. Aguillard* that "creation science" cannot be taught alongside evolution in public school science classes because the former is religion while the latter is science.

2001

A working draft of the entire human genome sequence is published following a decade-long private-public effort.

2003

The National Human Genome Research Institute publishes a comparison of human and chimpanzee genomes. Researchers find a high degree of overlap.

FOR FURTHER RESEARCH

Books

David Attenborough, *Life on Earth, a Natural History.* London: BBC/Collins, 1979.

Michael J. Behe, *Darwin's Black Box: The Biochemical Challenge to Evolution.* New York: Free Press, 1996.

Janet Browne, *Charles Darwin: The Power of Place.* Princeton, NJ: Princeton University Press, 2003.

Luigi Cavalli-Sforza et al., *The History and Geography of Human Genes.* Princeton, NJ: Princeton University Press, 1993.

Charles Darwin, *The Descent of Man, and Selection in Relation to Sex.* London, Murray, 1871.

Charles Darwin, *On the Origin of Species.* New York: E.P. Dutton, 1972.

Richard Dawkins, *The Blind Watchmaker: Why the Evidence of Evolution Reveals a Universe Without Design.* New York: W.W. Norton, 1986.

Richard Dawkins, *The Selfish Gene.* Oxford: Oxford University Press, 1976.

Daniel Dennett, *Darwin's Dangerous Idea: Evolution and the Meanings of Life.* New York: Simon & Schuster, 1996.

Michael J. Denton, *Evolution: A Theory in Crisis.* Bethesda, MD: Adler & Adler, 1986.

Jared Diamond, *The Third Chimpanzee: The Evolution and Future of the Human Animal.* New York: HarperCollins, 1992.

Theodosius Dobzhansky, *Evolution, Genetics, and Man.* New York: John Wiley & Sons, 1955.

Douglas J. Futuyama, *Science on Trial: The Case for Evolution.* Sunderland, MA: Sinauer Associates, 1997.

Duane T. Gish, *Creation Scientists Answer Their Critics.* El Cajon, CA: Institute for Creation Research, 1993.

Stephen Jay Gould, *The Panda's Thumb: More Reflections in Natural History.* New York, W.W. Norton, 1980.

Ken Ham, *The Lie: Evolution.* Green Forest, AR: Master Books, 1987.

Fred Hoyle and Chandra Wickramasinghe, *Evolution from Space.* New York: Simon & Schuster, 1981.

Sarah Blaffer Hrdy, *The Woman That Never Evolved.* Cambridge, MA: Harvard University Press, 1983.

Robert Jastrow, ed., *The Essential Darwin.* Boston: Little, Brown, 1984.

Phillip E. Johnson, *Defeating Darwinism by Opening Minds.* Downers Grove, IL: InterVarsity Press, 1997.

Philip Kitcher, *Abusing Science: The Case Against Creationism.* Cambridge, MA: MIT Press, 1982.

Ernst Mayr, *The Growth of Biological Thought: Diversity, Evolution, and Inheritance.* Cambridge, MA: Harvard University Press, 1982.

Geoffrey F. Miller, *The Mating Mind: How Sexual Choice Shaped the Evolution of Human Nature.* New York: Doubleday, 2000.

Henry M. Morris, ed., *Scientific Creationism,* 2d ed. Green Forest, AR: Master Books, 1985.

Ronald L. Numbers, *The Creationists: The Evolution of Scientific Creationism.* New York: Alfred A. Knopf, 1992.

Dean L. Overman, *A Case Against Accident and Self-Organization.* New York: Rowman & Littlefield, 1997.

Mark Pagel, ed., *Encyclopedia of Evolution.* New York: Oxford University Press, 2002.

Matt Ridley, *Evolution.* Boston: Blackwell, 2003.

John Maynard Smith, *The Theory of Evolution.* New York: Penguin, 1975.

Bryan Sykes, *The Seven Daughters of Eve.* New York: W.W. Norton, 2001.

Edward O. Wilson, *The Diversity of Life.* New York: W.W. Norton, 1999.

David Young, *The Discovery of Evolution.* New York: Cambridge University Press, 1992.

Carl Zimmer, *Evolution: The Triumph of an Idea.* New York: HarperCollins, 2002.

Periodicals

Frederick Crews, "Saving Us from Darwin," *New York Review of Books,* October 4, 2001.

Theodosius Dobzhansky and B. Spassky, "Evolutionary Changes in Laboratory Cultures of *D. Pseudoobscura,*" *Evolution*, vol. 1, 1947.

Leonid A. Gavrilov and Natalia S. Gavrilova, "Evolutionary Theories of Aging and Longevity," *Scientific World Journal,* February 7, 2002.

Stephen Jay Gould, "Is a New and General Theory of Evolution Emerging?" *Paleontology*, vol. 6, 1980.

Stephen Jay Gould and Richard C. Lewontin, "The Spandrels of San Marco and the Panglossian Paradigm: A Critique of the Adaptationist Programme," *Proceedings of the Royal Society*, 1979.

Richard Leakey and Alan Walker, "*Homo Erectus* Unearthed," *National Geographic*, November 1985.

Simon Conway Morris, "Rerunning the Tape," *Times* (London) *Literary Supplement*, December 13, 1991.

John Rennie, "15 Answers to Creationist Nonsense," *Scientific American*, July 2002.

John Maynard Smith, "Taking a Chance on Evolution," *New York Review of Books*, May 14, 1992.

Frank J. Sulloway, "Darwin and His Finches: The Evolution of a Legend," *Journal of the History of Biology*, vol. 15, 1982.

Robert Wright, "The Accidental Creationist: Why Stephen Jay Gould Is Bad for Evolution," *New Yorker*, December 13, 1999.

Web Sites

AboutDarwin.com, www.aboutdarwin.com. This Web site contains information on the life and works of Charles Darwin, including a chronology, photographs, and an account of his voyage.

Access Research Network, www.arn.org. An antievolution, pro–intelligent design site that includes profiles of many authors, an online forum, and books and tapes for sale.

American Institute of Biological Sciences, www.aibs.org. AIBS is the leading professional society for American biologists. It actively defends the teaching of evolution as a standard part of the curriculum.

Center for Science and Culture, www.discovery.org. An anti-evolutionary site sponsored by the Discovery Institute, it features the writings of many of the leading advocates of intelligent design.

Charles Darwin Foundation, www.darwinfoundation.org. This is the site of a nonprofit foundation working to restore and preserve the natural heritage of the Galápagos Islands.

Evolution: A Journey to Where We're from and Where We're Going, www.pbs.org. An online companion to the eight-hour Public Broadcasting Service series of the same name.

Institute for Creation Research, www.icr.org. This is the site of the strongly antievolutionist organization, the Institute for Creation Research, which is dedicated to the promotion of young-earth biblical literalism as science.

Institute of Human Origins, www.asu.edu. This site presents information on hominid fossils, a bibliography, and other useful information for those interested in evolution.

National Center for Science Education, www.natcenscied.org. This is the Web site of the nation's leading organization defending the teaching of evolution and critiquing the claims of antievolutionary creationists.

The Panda's Thumb, www.pandasthumb.org. This online forum

is dedicated to explaining the theory of evolution, critiquing the claims of the antievolution movement, and defending science and science education.

Talk.Origins Archive, www.talkorigins.org. This Web site provides a rich resource for question-and-answer style information about evolution from a mainstream scientific perspective.

The Origin of Species, www.literature.org. Charles Darwin's most famous book is available in full at this site.

University of California Museum of Paleontology, www.ucmp. berkeley.edu. This site includes online displays, a guide to geological time, and evolution resources.

Unofficial Stephen Jay Gould Archive, www.stephenjaygould.org. This Web site presents a large collection of writings by and about the controversial paleontologist who both defended and attacked Darwinism.

INDEX